ETHICS IN JOHN COBB'S
PROCESS THEOLOGY

American Academy of Religion
Academy Series

edited by
Susan Thistlethwaite

Number 62
ETHICS IN JOHN COBB'S PROCESS THEOLOGY

by
Paul Custodio Bube

Paul Custodio Bube

ETHICS IN JOHN COBB'S PROCESS THEOLOGY

Scholars Press
Atlanta, Georgia

ETHICS IN JOHN COBB'S
PROCESS THEOLOGY

by
Paul Custodio Bube

© 1988
The American Academy of Religion

Library of Congress Cataloging in Publication Data

Bube, Paul Custodio.
  Ethics in John Cobb's process theology / Paul Custodio Bube.
    p. cm. --(AAR academy series)
  Bibliography: p.
  ISBN 1-555-40271-2. ISBN 1-555-40272-0 (pbk.)
  1. Cobb, John B. 2. Christian ethics--History--20th century.
3. Process theology. I. Title. II. Series: American Academy of
Religion academy series.
BX4827.C6B83   1989
241'.092'4--dc19   88-30616

Printed in the United States of America
on acid-free paper

To my wife, Joni, and our daughter, Melissa Lee:
your patience and support encourage me;
your love enriches my life profoundly;
you manifest to me each day the presence of Christ,
the creative transformative power of God.

O magnify the LORD with me,
and let us exalt his name together!
Psalm 34:3

CONTENTS

PREFACE

The role of process thought, especially as formulated in the philosophy of Alfred North Whitehead, has become increasingly prominent in contemporary North American theology since its appropriation by the "empirical theologians" of Chicago Divinity School in the 1930's. At that time, process theology was isolated to the island of Chicago while the great wave of neo-orthodoxy crashed down upon the wreckage of American liberalism. But, by the end of the 1950's, the tide of neo-orthodoxy was receding as it lost its relevance to the secular, "post-modern" mind; and with it ebbed confidence in a wholly other, omnipotent divinity. In its wake sprouted the critique of the existentialist and secular theologians who only confirmed the incongruity of traditional Christian beliefs with contemporary experience. However, a second-generation of empirical theologians, who had weathered the storm of neo-orthodoxy, already were busy at the constructive task of re-presenting Christian beliefs in a manner coherent with contemporary experience. Two of these theologians, Schubert Ogden and John Cobb, emerged by the mid-1960's as leading spokespersons of what has become known as process theology.[1]

Ogden and Cobb have continued to extend the influence of process thought not only among academic theologians, but also among seminary students where they teach.[2] Consequently, they have received attention from German theologians, on the one hand, and, (as if a symbolic successor to secular theology), appeared on the front page of one of the largest U.S. newspapers, on the other.[3] Of the two, Cobb has probably been most active in disseminating the process message. His founding of the Center for Process Studies

with its journal, *Process Studies*, along with his personal involvement in numerous conferences involving thinkers from fields ranging
from comparative religions to sociology, biology and economics, has
opened up new vistas of questioning and possible syntheses of
thought beyond the limits of traditional academic theology.

Not surprisingly, one of those vistas has been the field of
ethics. There has been a growing interest in ethics in the recent work
of Ogden (1979; 1982) and Cobb (Birch & Cobb 1981; Cobb
1982b), in addition to a growing number of articles and books by
philosophers and theologians who are influenced by Whitehead.[4]
However, John Cobb's work stands out in this regard, if for no other
reason than his early attention to problems in ethical theory (e.g.,
1954; 1965a), as well as his more recent attention to ethical issues
such as ecology, political liberation, and economic justice.

Even so, Cobb has not yet systematized a comprehensive
theory of ethics—especially, a theological ethic. On the one hand,
there is some debate between Cobb and other process thinkers as to
how integral the Christian experience of faith is to Cobb's theology,
and hence, to his theological ethics. For example, Schubert Ogden
(1965) and David Tracy (1977) suggest that Cobb's theology is not
so much a *Christian* natural theology, as it is a natural theology
which works out the theological implications of Whitehead's philosophy. On the other hand, lack of a systematic exposition of
Cobb's theological ethics has led to some confusion about how best
to interpret Cobb's ethics. For example, Charles Reynolds suggests
that Cobb's ethics succeeds in appropriating a deontological understanding of obligation "by turning to Kant for assistance in dealing
with the issue of how we are to discern our moral obligations" (1977,
121). Whereas, in a discussion of Cobb's article, *The Political
Implications of Whitehead's Philosophy* (1981b), Franklin Gamwell
suggests that Cobb's contention that norms for social change are
grounded deontologically in the kind of change that should be sought
(i.e., creative synthesis), rather than in specific goals of change, is
not true to Cobb's overall intention and should be recast teleo-
logically to ground the norms for change in the goal of maximal
beauty (Gamwell 1981, 32 f.). The general goal of a critical and
systematic analysis of Cobb's theology and ethics is to elucidate and
clarify the explicit and implicit elements of Cobb's theological ethics
to help resolve these sorts of questions.

The more specific goals of this essay are to examine the relationship of Cobb's ethical reflections to his overall theological development and to evaluate critically Cobb's Christian ethics in light of traditional and modern Christian social ethics. I have taken as an important clue for understanding Cobb's ethical development his statement that in 1969 he became so acutely aware of the proportions of the ecological crisis that he "went through a conversion experience" which has profoundly changed his theology as well as his personal life (1981a, 74 f.). One could interpret Cobb's "conversion" merely as a recognition that the ecological crisis, like other issues, needed to be in addressed within the framework of his theological method. In analyzing and elucidating Cobb's social ethics, however, I will show that his conversion was not merely a recognition of the need to address the ecological crisis within the framework of his early theology, but that it included profound changes in both theological method and christology. Before 1969, Cobb's empirical method took as its starting point the Christian vision of the world, which he came to identify with the Christian structure of existence. The christology that grew out of this method was primarily what he himself called a "Jesusology," that is, an attempt to explain how the historical person, Jesus, decisively revealed God. After 1969, when Cobb acknowledged that both theology and ethics had become too disciplinary—too caught up with their own methodological questions—to give insight into the global ecological crisis, both Cobb's method and christology have become characterized by the notion of "creative transformation" in place of the Christian structure of existence. Hence, I examine and evaluate how creative transformation not only becomes the central category of Cobb's method and christology, but also the central norm for Cobb's understanding humanity's relationship to the environment, social justice, and political and economic liberation.

Chapters one and two examine how Cobb approaches the problem of theological method in relation to empirical theology, christology, and ethics before 1969. Chapter one examines the development of Cobb's method, "a Christian natural theology," which is concerned with the relationship between experience and religious beliefs. The chapter discusses the application of this method to beliefs about humanity and Christ and concludes with a preliminary assessment of the empirical character of Cobb's theological method, its relationship to christology, and cursory implications for ethics.

Just as Cobb's early method addresses the relationship of experience to religious beliefs, his early moral theory raises the question of the relationship of experience to moral principles. Chapter two discusses the empirical grounding of his formal ethics or metaethics and examines how Cobb develops his early moral theory in relation to obligation theory, value theory, and character theory, arguing that Cobb's central normative category is the Christian structure of existence.

Chapter three examines how Cobb's confrontation with the ecological crisis raises serious questions about the theological and ethical adequacy of the Christian structure of existence. In order to address the ecological crisis adequately, Cobb reformulates his christology which, in turn, leads to a substantial revision of his theological ethics as well as a transformation of theological method.

Finally, chapters four and five examine the emerging elements of Cobb's social-ecological ethics. Chapter four examines Cobb's understanding of the notions of rights and justice in light of criticisms raised against the ability of process theology to ground these notions. Chapter five examines whether Cobb's theological ethics, especially with its emphasis upon the issue of ecology, is able to support a praxis of political and economic liberation.

ᐤᐤᐤᐤᐤᐤ

There are a number of persons who have contributed their time, insights, and encouragement toward helping me complete this endeavor. I am grateful to the staff members of the Center for Process Studies in Claremont, California, who have been always generous and friendly in their assistance—often tracking down and providing copies of hard-to-find books, articles, and papers, which have been invaluable to my research.

Professor John B. Cobb, Jr., deserves special acknowledgment and thanks. Professor Cobb has been extremely gracious in commenting on rough drafts of several chapters and in making a number of his unpublished papers available to me. His generous and solicitous cooperation have deeply enriched me as a person and a Christian ethicist. I hope this essay has done justice to the insight and vision that I have found in his theological ethics.

Several persons at the School of Religion at the University of Southern California, where this essay began as a dissertation, deserve special thanks. Professor J. Wesley Robb has made a lasting contribution to my academic and personal growth by acting as teacher, counselor, and friend. Vera Collins, the Administrative Assistant of the School of Religion, managed to humanize the inevitable red tape that accompanies graduate study. I am grateful for the support and encouragement that I have received from my dissertation committee: Professors Dallas Willard, Donald E. Miller, and John P. Crossley, Jr., the chairperson of my committee. I am especially indebted to Professor Crossley for challenging me to think more carefully, to question more deeply, and for recommending that I publish this work.

I am thankful to Susan Thistlethwaite, the editor of the Academy Series, for providing many helpful suggestions for converting a dissertation into a book. Of course, I alone am to blame for any shortcomings in this final product.

Finally, I am most thankful to my wife, Joni, and our daughter, Melissa Lee, who have provided me with the time and motivation to complete this project.

Paul Custodio Bube
Kansas Wesleyan University
Summer, 1988

NOTES

1. Works such as *Christ Without Myth* (1961) and *The Reality of God* (1966) by Ogden, and *Living Options in Protestant Theology* (1962) and *A Christian Natural Theology* (1965a) by Cobb, were instrumental in bringing process theology to the forefront of theological dialogue in the 1960's.

2. Ogden teaches at Perkins Theological Seminary in Dallas, Texas, and Cobb teaches at the School of Theology at Claremont, California.

3. Cobb, in particular, has had several works translated into German, including *The Structure of Christian Existence* (1967b), *God and the World* (1969), and *Is It Too Late? A Theology of Ecology* (1972b). Ogden has been influential in propagating Bultmann's work in the United States, e.g., with his collection and translation of

Existence and Faith: Shorter Writings of Rudolf Bultmann (New York: Meridian Books, Inc., 1960). Moreover, Cobb, along with his colleague at the School of Theology at Claremont, David Griffin, were subjects of a front page *Los Angeles Times* article, Oct. 19, 1982, written by John Dart. In the article, Cobb is portrayed as approaching the problem of evil and suffering in a manner analogous to Rabbi Harold Kushner's *When Bad Things Happen to Good People* (1981). This article provoked over 100 letters to the *Times* in the following week (10% of the average number of all letters received in a given week).

4. David Griffin (1976) is perhaps the best known of the process thinkers writing on ethics. Newer thinkers such as Barbara Swyhart (1975) and Lynne Belaief (1984) are dealing with issues of bioethics and metaethics, respectively.

CHAPTER ONE

THEOLOGICAL METHOD BEFORE 1969

In order to understand the ethics in John Cobb's process theology, it is important first to gain a precise understanding of Cobb's theological method and how it applies to substantive issues—particularly to anthropology and christology which have special relevance to any Christian ethics. Hence, the task of this chapter is to analyze Cobb's pre-1969 understanding of the nature of theological method and its application to anthropology and christology. The next chapter deals with Cobb's pre-1969 understanding of ethics and its relationship to his theological method.

FORMULATING THE PROBLEM FOR METHOD

Cobb's initial theological development in the early 1950's was profoundly influenced by Alfred North Whitehead's "organismic" philosophy which dominated the theological empiricism of Cobb's alma mater, the Chicago School of Divinity, during his study there. The theological method that Cobb has worked out in this context, which he calls a "Christian natural theology," has been viewed by some theologians, such as Ogden (1965) and Tracy (1977), as little more than an attempt to revise and ground theological doctrines, such as the notion of divine omnipotence, in Whitehead's philosophy. Indeed, Ogden and Tracy argue that there is little reason to call Cobb's method a *Christian* natural theology, for his method appears to be primarily philosophical, and thus independent of all religious orientations. It would be better if Cobb were to avoid ambiguity and

1

acknowledge that his theology is a natural theology more akin to
Hartshorne's own rationalist undertaking (Hartshorne 1967). While
Ogden and Tracy are essentially correct in their recognition of the
prominence of Whitehead's thought in Cobb's method, I believe that
their criticisms fail to grasp fully the underlying foundation of
Cobb's Christian natural theology which, when viewed in the context
of his early development, is clearly a more profoundly Christian attempt at method than it may appear at first glance.

A close analysis of Cobb's justification for the method of
Christian natural theology, beginning with his dissertation, *The
Independence of Christian Faith from Speculative Beliefs* (1953a), and
worked out more systematically in *Living Options in Protestant
Theology: A Survey of Methods* (1962) and *A Christian Natural
Theology* (1965a), indicates that Cobb's fundamental aim extends
beyond mere Whiteheadian orthodoxy to incorporate some of the central insights found in empirical, rationalist and neo-orthodox approaches to method. Cobb's aim becomes clear when one takes note
of the initial problem he is trying to solve with theological method.
He indicates in his dissertation that he wants to outline a theological
method to resolve his own "fundamental religious problem," which,
for Cobb, is the problem of understanding and nurturing the grounds
of Christian faith so as to keep faith from being undermined by new
knowledge and experience, that is, from being contradicted by empirically verifiable propositions (1953a, ii). In *Living Options*, Cobb
formulates this problem in the wider context of the Christian
churches' confrontation with doctrinal relativism and secular thought
(1962, 8). Lack of agreement among the churches, the compelling
and conflicting values and views of secularism, and the inconsistency
of scientific thought with religious beliefs and doctrines show beliefs
and doctrines to be inherently relative or "speculative." Put differently, religious beliefs and doctrines appear to be no more than
"particular conclusions of thought which can be contradicted by
equally legitimate conclusions of thought" (1953a, ii). At the existential level, the problem for Cobb is that knowledge of the speculative or relative character of beliefs shakes (or potentially shakes)
confidence in their ultimate truth and thus calls into question the
grounds of Christian faith. The problem confronting theological
method, then, is whether there is a way to educe beliefs and doctrines

which are consistent with empirical knowledge and supportive of faith.

WORKING TOWARD THEOLOGICAL METHOD: LIVING OPTIONS

It is evident from the way that Cobb formulates the problem that he associates faith with religious experience, and belief with reason. Cobb acknowledges two general methodological alternatives for elucidating the relationship between faith and belief. On the one hand, there is a tradition in Protestantism that identifies faith with belief, or at least sees faith as dependent upon belief. This "Protestant rationalism" tends to assume that the truth of belief—and, thus, of faith—can be demonstrated by reason, which, conceived broadly, includes common sense and cosmology (cf. 1953a, 8 ff.). The other general alternative, rooted in "mainstream Protestantism," views faith as an attitude received from God and for the most part independent of reason and belief, though it gives certainty to belief (1953a, 3 ff.).

If faith is more or less identical to belief, as it is for the more extreme forms of Protestant rationalism, then faith is, in principle, dependent upon reason. If the grounds of faith are dependent upon the reasonableness of belief, then theological method must demonstrate how non-speculative beliefs can be formulated. Cobb sees three possible approaches to formulating belief rationally, and, hopefully, nonspeculatively: (a) by basing belief on common sense; (b) by basing belief on cosmology; and (c) by basing belief on value theory. For present purposes the first two can be combined under the heading of cosmology, since "the cosmologies of one age enter into the common sense of the next" (1953a, 31). The relation between belief and value theory will be discussed in the next chapter.

If faith is an attitude distinct from belief and initiated by the object of faith, as it is for mainstream Protestantism, then the object of faith is often thought of in either of two antithetical ways: either it is an integral part of our human experience and knowledge; or it is wholly independent from reason and belief (1962, chap. 5). The first alternative, which Cobb sees best exemplified by Henry Nelson Wieman's empirical theology, views the object of faith as wholly immanent in human experience. The second alternative, which Cobb sees best exemplified by Karl Barth's neo-orthodox theology, views the object of faith as radically transcending natural experience.1

Cobb's analysis of these options in theological method— cosmological, empirical, and neo-orthodox—focuses on the nature of God, which for Cobb, is the belief most central to Christian faith and most vulnerable to speculative grounding. Proof of the adequacy of a theological method, that is, a method that surmounts the problem posed by speculative belief, will be its ability to formulate a doctrine of God that nurtures faith and is not susceptible to contradiction by what is known with certainty.

The cosmological option in theological method attempts to derive a concept of God that follows rationally from the nature of the universe. Put differently, cosmology, as the philosophical attempt to give a rational, systematic account of the nature of the universe, provides rational grounds for belief in God. In order for cosmology to be able to provide a non-speculative grounding, it must be the "type of cosmology which claims to be the science of necessary truths," that is, it must be a metaphysics (Cobb 1953a, 30). Thus, insofar as religious beliefs can be shown to be metaphysically necessary, they can be considered non-speculative. (This sort of method is akin to the type of natural theology that Ogden and Tracy believe that Cobb has de facto worked out in *A Christian Natural Theology*.)

Cobb's general critique of cosmology and metaphysics in his dissertation, as well his criticism of the Thomist and Personalist attempts at grounding belief in cosmology (1962, Part 1), argue that a cosmological grounding for belief is inherently speculative because there are several valid, yet incompatible, cosmologies to choose from which give a systematic account of empirical facts (1953a, 36). More specifically, Cobb believes that metaphysics is ultimately elusive in light of Hume's analysis of causality which refutes the assumption that there can be any necessary causal relations between entities, thus "replac[ing] natural objective law with psychological, subjective law" (1953a, 16). Inasmuch as cosmology attempts to describe the laws governing the nature of things, no one cosmological system can be metaphysically true. Therefore, a cosmological grounding for beliefs is not sufficient for theological method because it cannot claim to be unequivocally true. Rather than summarizing Cobb's own critique of Thomism or Personalism, I believe it more illuminating to apply Cobb's general critique to Hartshorne's attempt at a metaphysical theology.

Hartshorne is quite confident of metaphysics' ability to provide a rational, non-speculative doctrine of God, and he has proposed his own natural theology based upon his metaphysical method (1967). Although, like Cobb, Hartshorne recognizes the pluralism of metaphysical systems that abound on the philosophical scene, unlike Cobb, he believes that it is possible to demonstrate that one metaphysical system is more consistent and coherent than all others: where there are "really two internally trouble-free but mutually incompatible systems, they must be alternative (empirically testable) specializations of a more general system which alone is metaphysical" (1970, 69). For example, where there are two contradictory metaphysical positions on the meaning of the term "perfection," Hartshorne argues that the contradictions can be overcome first, by clarifying the meaning that each system gives the term so that confused and indefinite meanings are eliminated; and second, by checking the consistency of the term with the overall system so as to revise the term (1970, 69-71). At the end of such analysis—which, of course, is a monumental task—Hartshorne believes we will come to one, true metaphysical system.

Although Cobb clearly has sympathy for Hartshorne's endeavor, (indicated by the parallels of his own view of God with Hartshorne's), his critique of cosmology indicates that he does not accept the metaphysical ground as sufficient for the problem of faith. The problem with metaphysics is that Marxian criticism, sociology of knowledge, and psychoanalysis have demonstrated that rationality itself is influenced by economic, social and unconscious factors which create doubt about the ability of reason in general to attain objectivity (1953a, 34 f.). Even with self-critical awareness of the short-comings of reason, metaphysics can only approximate necessary truths. Thus, even the sort of analyses proposed by Hartshorne, though necessary and valuable, is not sufficient to provide a non-speculative grounding for belief. Moreover, we may note that the contention that two incompatible metaphysical systems can be subsumed under a more general, necessary system, itself appears speculative, for the multitude of competing cosmologies on today's scene indicate that Hartshorne's contention is not based upon what is demonstrably the case, but rather on what is hoped to be true. Hence,

Cobb's rejection of any metaphysics, even Hartshorne's, as the basis of a natural theology follows upon the inability of metaphysics to account unequivocally for the nature of the world.

Nonetheless, although rejecting metaphysics and cosmology as the sufficient grounding of belief, Cobb obviously sees a necessary role for cosmology in theological method. The nature of this role and the reasons why Cobb argues for its necessity become clearer after examining the two other options in method, namely, the empirical and neo-orthodox.

The empirical option, unlike the cosmological, views faith and its object as a component of human experience rather than as a product of reasoned belief or an a priori principle. Wieman's efforts in empirical analysis and description of human experience to discern that reality which evokes faith exemplifies this option. Wieman argues that empirical analysis of human experience shows that all types of experiencing involve the experience of some meaning belonging to concrete events (1963, 5). The source of the meaningfulness of events is experienced as creativity or the creative good. However, Wieman's empiricism is limited to merely describing the source of events of meaning, and thus, Wieman must identify God either with the description of the events themselves or with what is abstractly common to those events. Wieman's view of God, as Cobb notes, includes "nothing concrete transcending experience" (Cobb 1953a, 88).

At this point, Cobb points out that the key problem with this sort of empirical theology is that its restriction to mere description of experience does not account for the reality of the object of experience. Because that which is not perceived as ontologically concrete cannot elicit devotion, Wieman must presuppose an ontology, thus a cosmology, if his description of the object of faith is to evoke loyalty and commitment (1962, 117). By ignoring the ontological question in hopes of being more strictly empirical, Wieman nonetheless must assume either that "events are themselves . . . ontologically ultimate, or that they are . . . manifestations of another type of reality underlying them (substances? persons? material entities?)" (Cobb 1969c, 93). Either way, Wieman makes a cosmological, and thus a speculative, assumption.

Even if we were to acknowledge that the astuteness of Wieman's description somehow avoids the ontological question, his view of God is inadequate to evoke and nurture faith. If God refers to individual concrete events, it is problematic that God can sustain loyalty and commitment, because either God is a plurality of events incapable of giving direction and unity to loyalty, or if God is a concrete unity, God's nature, like a discrete concrete event, is transitory, thus incapable of nurturing commitment (1953a, 93 f.). If, however, the creative good refers to what is common to creative events, then God is an ideal abstracted from all creative events and thus has no actuality. Although abstract ideals such as economic or political ideologies often elicit loyalty, recognition that such ideals are abstractions from human experience usually weakens loyalty or else subordinates it to that which these ideals serve in concrete, human experience, namely, persons (1953a, 95 ff.; 1962, 115 f.). Thus, even if we allow that Wieman's empirical theology avoids speculation and offers a "living option" in theological method, Wieman's brand of empiricism reduces God and persons to abstractions from transient events, which is at best a "post-Christian" vision of existence (1962, 115, 321).

If belief in God cannot be grounded in cosmology without avoiding speculation, and if faith cannot be evoked or sustained by purely empirical description of the creative good, then the question arises whether faith transcends reason and experience altogether and finds its ground in a wholly other object. This neo-orthodox option, exemplified by Barth, understands faith solely as the result of God's grace. In faith we encounter God as Person, but this understanding of God is not dependent upon any ontological pre-understanding (1962, 173). In fact, as witnessed by Barth's famous *"Nein!"* to Emil Brunner's proposal for a Christian natural theology, Barth vehemently denies any possibility of human influence upon faith. Thus, the belief that God is Person comes only through God's self-revelation, which is wholly independent of human desire or preparation for it. Moreover, even the individual's response to God's revelation is a predicate of God's sovereign activity (1962, 185). Hence, where Protestant rationalism tends to reduce faith to speculative belief, Barth appears to reduce belief to faith originating in God's gracious act.

Methodologically, Barth works within the closed circle of God's self-revelation. For Barth, God's self-revelation is Jesus Christ, the Word of God which reconciles humanity to God. This

Word comes to humanity through Scripture, the sole purpose of which is to witness to Jesus Christ (1962, 180). Barth asserts that this understanding of the relationship of the Word of God to Jesus Christ and Scripture itself comes through the Bible. Thus, the hermeneutic principle for understanding Scripture is contained within Scripture; that is, it is contained in God's self-revelation in Jesus Christ to which Scripture witnesses.

Consequently, theology for Barth is "Dogmatics." It is concerned with the conformity of the church's proclamation of faith to the Scriptures, that is, to Jesus Christ the Word of God (1962, 181). Barth rejects any norm or data for theology other than the Word of God. Thus, he rejects any normative role in theology for human experience or reason, although these influence the language by which we communicate the church's proclamation (1962, 181).

Cobb sees three possible interpretations of Barth's theological method at this point: (a) Barth can be seen as surreptitiously working with a preunderstanding of the world and human experience which guides him in interpreting the Bible for our time; (b) Barth can be viewed as operating within a closed circle of revelation in which the Bible as the Word of God provides its own principles of interpretation which have no implications for topics other than God's revelation in Jesus Christ; or (c) Barth can be interpreted as acknowledging that the Bible provides its own principles of interpretation but that these principles lead to implications for understanding the wider world outside of revelation (1962, 197).

Some theologians, such as Daniel Day Williams, accuse Barth of presupposing a cosmology in which time and eternity are totally discontinuous, which in turn affects Barth's reading of what Scripture has to say about the reality of redemption in human society (see Williams 1949, 36-38). Although Cobb is not unsympathetic to this criticism and believes that Barth's exegesis does appear dependent upon a certain preunderstanding based upon fear of the consequences of any theological method open to natural theology, Cobb, nevertheless, is willing to accept Barth at face value (1962, 195 f.). For example, one can follow Barth in affirming that the radical dualism between God and humanity is not derived from a dualistic cosmology, but is known only in God's gracious self-disclosure, which, in reconciling the sinner to God, reveals the radical separation between the sinner and God. Such a claim on Barth's part is not a claim about cosmology, but only about the relationship between the individual and God which is revealed in Christ.

If theological method is viewed as operating within a closed circle of God's self-revelation, this method does prevent the undermining of faith by empirical knowledge and experience because faith is of a radically different order from knowledge and belief. Put differently, that which exists and is known outside of God's self-revelation, such as sinful humanity or nonhuman creation, either is nothingness, rejected and negated by God, or is unimportant (1962, 190 f.). But if, as this interpretation holds, faith is viewed as discontinuous with the rest of human experience and knowledge, nothing could nurture or encourage the deepening of faith outside the event of revelation itself. Commenting on a similar interpretation of faith in Tillich's notion of "ecstasy," Cobb notes that although such an interpretation does not theoretically contradict or oppose knowledge and experience, it would existentially encourage doubt, for example, as to whether the revelation were merely subjective rather than originating in an objective reality (1953a, 125). Hence, Cobb concludes that this interpretation of Barth is theoretically a living option for method, but one he finds existentially closed for those who do not experience faith as completely discontinuous with the rest of living and thinking (1962, 321).

If, however, faith is not discontinuous with experience and knowledge, then how one understands the relationship of faith to experience and knowledge, (and more specifically how beliefs are formulated), will affect the development of faith. This alternative leads to the third possible interpretation, which Cobb believes to be the most promising for theological method. Like the previous view of method, this possibility takes as its starting point revelation, which Cobb calls elsewhere a "trans-subjective miracle" whence faith emerges (1953a, 124). Because faith originates independently of the relativities of speculative beliefs about the object of faith, it is not undermined by recognizing the speculative character of beliefs. But, because faith is existentially related to experience and knowledge, theological method must concern itself with a comprehensive and systematic view of that relationship. If any comprehensive and systematic understanding of the nature of experience and knowledge implies a cosmology, a fortiori a systematic understanding of the relationship of faith to experience and knowledge has cosmological

implications. Therefore, theological method, if it is to elucidate the
implications of revelation for other aspects of living requires speculative cosmology, and thus includes natural theology. Such a natural
theology would be dependent upon revelation, not vice versa. This is
why Cobb wants to call his method a *Christian* natural theology.

It is helpful to quote Cobb's own summary of this interpretation of Barth:

> If, finally we can allow the Bible to provide its own
> principles of interpretation but find that these lead to
> an inclusion in theology of topics other than God's
> self-revelation in Jesus Christ, then we must concern
> ourselves, *on the basis of revelation*, with the ques-
> tions that agitate the wider world of thought .... If
> carried through, it would lead to a synthesis of all
> knowledge through a philosophy selected, corrected,
> informed, and guided by the Christian faith. This is
> what we have called a Christian philosophy or sup-
> porting a Christian natural theology (1962, 197,
> italics added).

Cobb's existential conviction that revelation does have implications for our understanding of the world leads him to affirm the
foregoing interpretation of Barth as a model for Christian natural theology. Moreover, we can discern in this interpretation a general outline of Cobb's own constructive proposal for method. First, Cobb
holds that theological method must begin with Christian experience
or a Christian vision of the world (1953b, 222; 1962, 315 f.). This
is not to say theology must begin with any particular set of intellectual beliefs and doctrines; rather it must begin with what is fundamental to faith itself, namely, "the initial pre-conscious interpretation
of the data on the basis of which the intellectual structure is articu-
lated" (1969b, 119).[2] In *Living Options*, Cobb implies that this
vision can be discovered in part by analyzing what is common to the
spectrum of Protestant theologies (1962, 315 f.). In an earlier article,
however, he explicitly identifies this starting point with the
"primitive interpretations of Christian experience [found in the Bible]
unconditioned by relativizing factors [social, historical, economic,
biographical]—an abstract ideal"—but an ideal which Cobb believes
can provide the theologian with guidance in formulating beliefs for

today (1953b, 222 f.). These primitive interpretations, which seem to be the closest we come to non-speculative beliefs, are the clearest and most profound articulation of faith and are distinguished by the central role they give to Christ (1953b, 219).

Second, theological method requires a cosmology coherent with these primitive interpretations of Christian experience, for "if these data are to be systematized consistently with one another and with all other human knowledge, they must be stated in relation to, and in terms of, an adequate and consistent interpretation of all facts, that is, an adequate philosophy" (1953b, 222 f.). (Of course, Cobb believes that Whitehead's cosmology best meets this criterion.) Hence, faith itself demands that theological method avail itself of cosmology, for to ignore the need to choose consciously a cosmology is to leave the cosmological implications of faith unconscious and uncriticized (1953a, 134; 1965a, 263). Moreover, choosing a cosmology on the basis of its coherence with the Christian vision is not a violation of reason, because the fact that there are a number of competing, legitimate cosmologies indicates that the grounds for choosing a cosmology lie outside reason in a more fundamental or "existential" vision (1953a, 139). Which vision one begins with should also be made as conscious and explicit as possible, and thus open to criticism on existential grounds.

Finally, Cobb holds that the aim of theological method is not to create or prove the truth of Christian faith, for faith is a "response to a revelatory miracle" (1953a, 136); rather, the aim of method is to "facilitate [faith], or to remove impediments to it" (1953a, 137). As such, Christian natural theology is not primarily concerned with the apologetic task of appealing to universal grounds to demonstrate the truth of the Christian faith to the non-believer, but with the task of removing obstacles which impede the doubter, that is, the task of nurturing the faith of one whose convictions are in tension with other aspects of life (1953b, 214). The aim of theology then is neither that of dogmatic proclamation, as it is with Barth, nor of rationalist or empiricist proof, as it is with Hartshorne and Wieman.

This aim limits the role that philosophy, and thus cosmology, plays in theological method as compared to that claimed for method by traditional natural theology or apologetics. Christian natural theology acknowledges that equally legitimate or valid cosmologies can account for all known facts of the universe, and so chooses a cosmology on the basis of its congruence with the experience of revelation, its coherence with empirical knowledge, and its philosophical excellence (1953a, 138; 1965a, 264). However, it must be noted that the self-conscious starting point of faith is not uncritical or literal acceptance of the Bible. In fact, much of modern doubt results from the inconsistency of biblical accounts of the world with the modern social and scientific accounts. The starting point is the shared Christian vision of reality that gave rise to the New Testament. To approximate this datum, the biblical "accounts must be purified of relativizing factors before they can constitute binding data. [Thus], *the ideal data for Christian theology are interpretive expressions of Christian experience which are free of determination by cultural, social and peculiarly personal factors*" (1953b, 217, Cobb's italics).

I believe that Cobb is essentially correct in holding that a notion such as a Christian vision of the world is basic to Christian experience and, hence, to theological method. But, it must be noted that such a basis is problematic, both because of the difficulty of transcending "cultural, social and peculiarly personal factors," and because pre-conscious Christian experience, by definition, cannot be made fully explicit so as to provide an unambiguous starting point for method. Cobb seems to be aware of this problem and accepts that the ideal data for theology can only be approximated and never finally attained, and thus will not eliminate diversity and pluralism among beliefs. Nonetheless, if it can be agreed upon that there is such a starting point, however difficult to articulate, the possibility of greater synthesis of belief than now exists is at least open.

Cobb's understanding of the limitation of cosmology and his confidence that faith is experienced as a transubjective reality account for Cobb's differences with Ogden and Tracy over use of the terminology "Christian natural theology" instead of "natural theology." Ogden and Tracy want to assign a more fundamental role to philosophy than does Cobb. For instance, Ogden claims that there is no "other standard than its philosophical excellence which enables us to decide for a certain form of natural theology" (1965, 115); and Tracy argues that "one has a clear (i.e., unambiguous) sense of the kind of evidence appealed to in natural theology when one simply states that philosophical evidence alone is applicable here" (1977, 32). Cobb, however, is not only concerned with "philosophical excellence," but also with showing the coherence between a particular existential experience of faith and empirical knowledge. Moreover, both Ogden and Tracy are assuming, like Hartshorne, that one cosmology can be demonstrated as more valid than all others on philosophical grounds; whereas, Cobb believes that we must accept the given plurality of valid cosmologies, and hence their speculative character. In short, Ogden and Tracy want to argue that cosmology is both necessary and sufficient for theological method, whereas Cobb, although recognizing the necessity of cosmology for any theological method that is going to nurture faith, rejects the contention that cosmology can be sufficient for method, because cosmology requires speculation and is always relative.

THE APPLICATION OF METHOD: A CHRISTIAN NATURAL THEOLOGY

To sum up, Cobb's Christian natural theology has three general criteria: (a) it takes as its primary datum or starting point what is central to the Christian vision, namely, the abstract ideal of the primitive witness of Christian faith expressed in the New Testament; (b) in order to relate the datum to contemporary knowledge and experience, it employs a cosmology which is philosophically excellent, consistent with empirical knowledge, and coherent with Christian experience (as that is discerned in the primitive witness); and (c) it has as its aim to nurture and help remove obstacles to faith. If Cobb's criteria for theological method are accepted, two questions arise about his actual execution of a Christian natural theology: "What is the Christian primitive witness to God's revelation?" and, "Why is Whitehead's cosmology more suitable for carrying out the task of a Christian natural theology than one of the other philosophically valid cosmologies?" The answer to the first question seems to depend upon whether we can discover the essential nature of Christianity. The answer to the second question cannot be discovered as directly or completely; rather, it depends upon how well Whitehead's philosophy can help us to overcome actual, specific obstacles to modern faith, including those which arise from interpreting the primitive witness for today. Hence, in examining how Cobb begins to answer these questions, I will look first at what Cobb takes

to be the essence of Christian vision, namely, the "Christian structure of existence" that grows out of the experience of God in Jesus
Christ.[3] Then I will look at how Cobb employs Whitehead's philosophy to help illumine two specific obstacles to modern faith that
arise from the centrality of Jesus Christ in the primitive witness of
faith: how the historical Jesus can mediate God's presence nearly
2000 years later; and how Jesus is related to God.

THE CHRISTIAN STRUCTURE OF EXISTENCE

Although Cobb suggests that historical analysis is a separate
method from Christian natural theology (1967b, 8), the primacy he
gives to the primitive witness of faith in the New Testament makes
historical analysis propaedeutic to Christian natural theology. Hence,
in order to approximate the nature of the primitive witness of
Christian faith, theology must avail itself of historical studies,
specifically historical analysis of the New Testament and Christian
tradition. Although recognizing the problem of historical relativism,
Cobb assumes that there is some objective reality of past events, and
that they are not merely an aspect of present observation (1965b,
270). Thus, the relativity of the historian's statement presupposes a
real, objective past. This means that Cobb recognizes that the theologian's understanding is abstracted and simplified from the past
reality and does not provide a wholly objective and neutral account of
the primitive witness of faith as it existed in the self-understanding of
the New Testament writers; however, such abstraction and simplifi-
cation is necessary and useful if there is to be any knowledge of a
past made up of manifold moments of human experience (1967b, 18
f.).

In short, Cobb looks upon the Bible as an historical docu-
ment that reflects the "relativizing factors" of social, economic, and
biographical situations of its writers (1953b, 212). Nevertheless, he
believes that in spite of these relativizing factors there is an essence
or "finality" to Christian faith which it is the goal of historical analysis to approximate. Drawing upon the resources of phenomen-
ology, Cobb focuses his analysis upon human nature as it has been
affected socially and historically and believes that the essence of
Christianity is a "structure of human existence" that has arisen out of
the Christian experience of faith, but which stands as one type of ex-

istence among many that have evolved in conjunction with human-kind's biological and historical development (Cobb 1967b, 17).

Cobb, following Heidegger, takes "existence" to be roughly the equivalent of the psyche or soul (1967b, 32), but which also connotes what the human subject is to her or himself, including conscious and unconscious reflections and feelings (1967b, 16). Put differently, the structure of human existence is the organizing matrix of conscious and unconscious human experience. Contrary to Heidegger, Cobb does not believe that the structure of human existence is universal and relatively fixed; rather it varies from culture to culture, and from age to age (1967b, 17).

One important example of such a structure of existence is what Karl Jaspers refers to as the "axial" human (1967b, 52). Expanding on Jaspers, Cobb points out that during the period between 800 B.C.E. and 200 B.C.E., a threshold between mythic consciousness and reflective consciousness was crossed by dominant segments of the populations of the five great centers of civilization—China, India, Persia, Greece and the Middle East (1967b, 52-54). Consequently, the organizing matrix of human existence became characterized by a shift from a reflective consciousness in the service of unconsciously produced symbols to a reflective consciousness in the service of itself and alienated from the unconscious (1967b, 54). Cobb notes that axial existence was accompanied both by a growing awareness of individuality and identity as reflective consciousness became unified, and by a growing sense of freedom or independence as reflective consciousness began to take control of the unconscious symbols that regulated thought and action (1967b, 55-57).

At the heart of the scriptural portrayal of Christian existence is the identification of a new existence as initiated by and rooted in Jesus Christ.[4] Preliminary then to the task of determining the structure of Christian existence, we need to attempt to reconstruct the structure of Jesus' existence—even if only asymptotically—for it is his existence which has given rise to the experience of Christian faith. Jesus of Nazareth was born into axial existence as that had been modified by the prophetic structure of existence (1967b, 110-12). When, in the eighth century B.C.E., the Hebrews began to enter into axial existence, their experience of Yahweh as a tribal deity was transformed into an experience of God as the one universal creator (1966, 130). In particular, a new seat of existence was formed out of the prophets' (especially Jeremiah's) experience of Yahweh as the One who elects individuals and confronts them with both demand and promise (1967b, 100). In this confrontation, the individual was forced to see her or himself as an "I" who consciously wills and decides in response to a personal demand, rather than simply as one who rationally orders one's experience of the world (1967b, 102 f.). In other words, in the individual's encounter with God, rational consciousness was confronted with the decision to be subject neither to itself as rationality nor to unconsciously derived symbols (for God has no image), but to a personal "I." What emerged was the structure of existence of "responsible personhood" which transcended and took responsibility for rational consciousness and mythic unconsciousness (1967b, 103-5).

Although the prophets themselves experienced God as present and active, the post-exilic inheritors of the new ethical consciousness were frustrated both in their ability to achieve righteousness in obedience to God's demands and in their hope to see the fulfillment of God's promise of a new day. Thus, they experienced God as "silent and remote" (1976, 110). God was experienced by some, such as the Pharisees, as One who ordained a sacred law in the past, and by others, such as the Essenes, as One who will establish a holy kingdom in the future (1966, 130). Not surprisingly, Jesus inherited the prophetic structure of existence in both its Pharisaic and apocalyptic modes. However, where the prophets had spoken *for* God, the New Testament portrays Jesus as speaking *from* God with such personal authority that he so transformed both the Pharisaic and apocalyptic modes of prophetic existence, that his demand for righteousness went beyond moral obedience to love, and his proclamation of the coming of God's kingdom brought the kingdom near (1966, 132). Cobb attributes Jesus' unique authority to an awareness of God which was so immediate and so pervasive that he actually existed "from God and for God" (1966, 132). Put differently, Jesus' apprehension of God was itself the organizing matrix of his self, the seat of his existence. Thus, out of the immediacy of his experience of God, Jesus transcended and fulfilled personal existence formed over against God as One who demands and promises, with a new existence, wholly identified with God as One who loves.

Although Jesus' words and activities were a reflection of his close identity with God, it was not until the early Christian community's experience of Jesus in the resurrection that they recognized God's presence in Jesus (1967b, 116). This radical experience evoked a new structure of existence that is not identical to Jesus' existence, but rather is measured by it. Jesus experienced God's nearness with personal immediacy, whereas the early Christians experienced God as near through and in Jesus Christ. Thus, although Jesus' confidence in the imminent coming of God's kingdom grew out of Jesus' personal experience of God's immediacy, the Christian community's confidence in the imminence of God's kingdom was a result of their experience of the risen Jesus (1967b, 116).

In the New Testament, the Christian community's new relationship with God in Christ is portrayed as the experience of the empowering presence of God's Spirit or the Spirit of Christ. This experience of the Spirit is neither a reversion to an archaic structure of existence in which reflective consciousness is submerged in the unconscious, nor a recapitulation of ethical consciousness. Rather, the experience of the Spirit of Christ transforms the responsible self into a radically self-transcending self, thus transforming the possibility of an existence fulfilled in obedience and righteousness into an existence fulfilled in agapic love (1967b, 133 ff.). This "spiritual existence fulfilled in love" transcends personal existence because where the prophetic structure of existence centers on one's acceptance of responsibility for one's activities, and thus brings an inward awareness of one's self as a deciding self or person, the Christian structure of existence, because it arises out of the experience of the inward state as the locus of God's activity, centers on responsibility for one's motives and attitudes, and thus brings an awareness of oneself as transcending one's self (1967b, 119-21). In other words, with the emergence of spiritual existence "the self became responsible for the choice of the center from which it organized itself and not only for what it chose from a given center" (1967b, 123). Thus, the Christian structure of existence includes and transcends the prophetic acceptance of the self's responsibility for one's actions—it is fulfilled in faith and love rather than obedience, hope rather than sectarian purity.[5]

THE FINALITY OF JESUS CHRIST

The primitive witness of Christian faith tells the modern theologian little more about the source of faith, that is, Jesus Christ, than that he was experienced as one who was closely identified with God, and that he was experienced so profoundly and intimately as Spirit—even as transcending death—that the Christian entered into a new structure of existence. If one accepts that the essence of the Christian witness is the self-transcending self fulfilled in love that arose historically out of this encounter with Jesus, one is still faced with several problems about how we are to conceive the nature of Jesus' profound effect on others, both during the first century and today. It is the role of christology to elucidate such questions. In order to point to some features of Cobb's christology and its relationship to his method, I will examine how he attempts to resolve two of these problems.

The first problem is explaining how it is possible for the twentieth century Christian to experience Jesus today, because if the Christian experience of God comes through Jesus, the theologian needs to give an account of how a person who lived almost 2000 years ago can have any actual relationship to the present experience. Even if the first problem is resolved, there remains a second problem of how it is possible for an infinite God to be decisively present in finite human being. Both of these questions, if not answered satisfactorily, present obstacles to modern faith by calling into doubt the basis of the Christian witness. In order to work out a christology that adequately articulates the meaning of the primitive witness for today's Christian, Cobb turns to cosmology.[6]

Many Christians today, like their early counterparts, claim that their faith grows out of a personal encounter with Jesus. Cobb recognizes that the question of how Jesus can have an actual effect on our present lives is part of the larger question of what causation is (1966, 148). Specifically, Cobb draws upon Whitehead who argues that all reality consists of actual occasions or moments of experience which are "events" that are "internally" or organically related to past events. Put differently, in a manner analagous to the way one's present awareness is largely constituted by conscious and unconscious memories of past events, an actual occasion is largely made up of its "prehensions" (or "feelings") of previous occasions of experience, so that an actual occasion's relationships to other actual occasions (other than contemporaries) are constitutive of what that actual entity (event) is. "Apart from [these] relationship[s], the event would not be itself" (Whitehead 1925, 123), and thus, insofar as a present occasion is constituted by its internal relations to past actual occasions, it can be said that those past occasions have causal efficacy for the present occasion (cf. Whitehead 1978, 19).

Drawing upon this understanding of causal efficacy as the way past actual occasions are prehended by a present occasion, Cobb notes that the relationship between cause and effect is the relationship between something that no longer exists to something that exists. Moreover, on the basis of relativity theory, such as Einstein's or Whitehead's, causal relations cannot exist among contemporary occasions because contemporary occasions are defined as those occasions which do not enter into each others' prehensions (Whitehead 1978, 65 f.; Cobb 1966, 149 f.). Therefore "the cause is always in the past of the effect, [which] means that something that no longer exists, and indeed only something that no longer exists, has efficacy in the present" (Cobb 1966, 150). Put differently, the concresence— the coming to be actual—of an actual occasion of experience is in part constituted by its prehension of past actual occasions, but the concrescing occasion is discrete and discontinuous from all past occasions. This understanding is substantiated by quantum theory of subatomic particles (see Whitehead 1925, chap. VIII). If all causes are non-existent occasions, then there does not appear to be any qualitative difference between the causal efficacy of an event that resides in the proximate past and an event lying in a more remote past (Cobb 1966, 151). Such a theory not only accords well with what we know from the modern understanding of sub-atomic particles, it also offers insight into experiences such as the vivid return of childhood memories, reports of mental telepathy, and memories of previous lives, without dismissing these experiences as phantasms, or appealing to problematic notions such as a collective unconscious and reincarnation (1966, 151-53). Thus, assuming Jesus to have been a real person who had causal efficacy upon the early Christians, it is possible, and even plausible, that Jesus can have causal efficacy for modern persons, and that "an attitude of expectancy, attention, and belief would be likely to facilitate such prehension" (1966 , 154).

Many modern Christians, like their early counterparts, not only claim that they have been deeply affected by the person of Jesus, but that they have also experienced God in Jesus. This claim raises the problem of how God was present in Jesus of Nazareth. Unless this belief can be conceived in a way that does not contradict experience and knowledge, it can become a serious obstacle to faith. Traditionally, Christians have answered the second question in terms of the incarnation of God in Jesus Christ. The meaning of the incarnation is unquestionably one of the most difficult beliefs for the Christian theologian to elucidate in a way that does not end up as purely speculative, reductionistic, or dogmatic.

Even in the earliest formulations of this doctrine there was heated debate over what it means to say that God became flesh in Jesus. Early Christians were divided into two major schools of thought: the Antiochine, which begins with the fact of Jesus' humanity and tries to articulate how God acted in Jesus; and the Alexandrine, which begins with the fact of God's presence in Jesus and tries to articulate how Jesus could be human (1966, 139). The latter school is often associated with the patristic doctrine of the impersonal humanity of Jesus, namely, that Jesus lived not as an individual person, but as humanity in the generic sense (Wolf 1958, 50). But if recent New Testament study has learned anything about Jesus, it is that he was an individual person (Wolf 1958, 50). Affirming Jesus' individual personality, Cobb prefers to approach this issue in the tradition of the Antiochine school which he believes "lost out" to the Alexandrine school because it lacked the "conceptuality for explaining how God could at his own initiative be genuinely present to and in a man without displacing some element in the personal humanity of that man" (1966, 139). Hence, he turns to Whitehead's cosmology for a more adequate conceptuality to understand God's relationship to the actual individual, Jesus.

Central to Cobb's understanding of God's relation to Jesus is Whitehead's understanding of God's relation to the actual world in general, and human beings in particular. Whitehead believes that essential to the nature of God is God's operation in the actual world as a principle of concretion or limitation (1925, 174; 1978, 343 f.). Cobb notes that as the principle of concretion, God is primordial, providing to each emerging occasion of experience an eternal ordering of possibilities for actualization. These possibilities or "eternal objects" are, like the primordial nature of God, unchanging (1965a, 155). Expanding on Whitehead, Cobb suggests that God as primordial envisions an indefinite number of eternal objects such that "every possible state of the actual world is already envisioned as possible .... Thus, the one primordial ordering of eternal objects is relevant to every actuality with perfect specificity" (1965a, 155 f.). This view reinforces Whitehead's emphasis upon freedom in the process of concrescence by recognizing that God determines not one possible future, but makes possible many possible futures; and at the same time preserves the notion that God provides order to the universe. Put differently, God primordially and eternally determines all possible actualizations which each individual occasion of experience may choose in its concresence.

The question that arises from this view of God's primordial nature is, How can an eternal ordering be relevant for a concrete occasion in a given moment of experiencing (1965a, 155)? Whitehead himself did little to answer this question except to say that God makes available a scaled set of relevant eternal objects to each concrescing occasion by providing the occasion with an "initial aim" toward satisfaction or fulfillment (1965a, 153 f.). However, this does not explain how actual occasions "feel"—or more appropriately, "prehend"—this aim. Put differently, How does an actual occasion "know" which, of all the possibilities envisioned by God, are those which are relevant to its actualization (cf. Whitehead 1978, 249)?

Cobb suggests that God makes relevant to an occasion the scaled set of eternal objects out of which it forms its subjective aim by entertaining for the new occasion the aim for the occasion's ideal satisfaction (1965a, 156). This "entertainment" consists of God's feeling of a "proposition of which the novel occasion is the logical subject and the appropriate eternal object is the predicate" (1965a, 156). That is, God, in accord with God's own eternal aim at actualization or "strength of beauty," actualizes Godself in each moment so as to influence each actual occasion with an appetition toward ideal actualization (1965a, 182). This is analogous to the way that a human actual occasion actualizes itself to influence other occasions, whether it be to move the hand muscles in its body, or to evoke certain behavior in future occasions of other persons (1965a, 182). Thus, God functions in the self-constitution of each occasion in a similar manner that other actual occasions do: God, along with all other entities in a novel occasion's past, is prehended by the new occasion. Hence, those past entities which include propositional feelings with a subjective form of desire for actualization are prehended by the new occasion so that its own aim at actualization will be "some synthesis or adaptation of these aims for which it is itself finally responsible" (1965a, 185). However, God's propositional feelings are the most fundamental for the new occasion because they include the locus and extension of the occasion's standpoint (1965a, 183), and because they are the most relevant, that is, the ideal, aim for the occasion.

This elaboration of Whitehead relies upon the importance that Cobb places on the consequent nature of God in Whitehead's philosophy as well as upon his re-interpretation of God as a personal society rather than as one actual entity. Wieman and some of the more empirically minded theologians from the Chicago School of Divinity reject Whitehead's view of the consequent nature of God as speculative and unnecessary to his overall philosophy. Neither Cobb nor Whitehead himself would deny that the view of the consequent nature of God is speculative; however, they would both affirm its necessity to the categoreal scheme. This is because Whitehead's method is to construct a cosmology that is coherent, that is, a cosmology whose "fundamental ideas, in terms of which the scheme is developed, presuppose each other so that in isolation they are meaningless" (Whitehead 1978, 3). This requires that no principle, especially God, is "to be treated as an exception to all metaphysical principles, invoked to save their collapse" (1978, 343). God's having a consequent nature follows from these requirements, because for God to have causal efficacy, God must be an actual entity (cf. Whitehead 1978, 24); and in order to be an actual entity, God must have a physical pole that corresponds to the mental pole that is the primordial nature. This physical pole is made up of God's physical feelings of the actual world, "consequent upon the creative advance of the world" (1978, 343-45). Without the consequent nature of God, it would be difficult to conceive of God (viewed as merely primordial) as entertaining propositional feelings that are relevant to the actual world of the new occasion.

Moreover, for God's feelings of the world to correspond to each new moment, God must be a personal order of actual occasions. As such, God's prehensions of the world are cumulative and thus change according to the creative advance of the world. There is some debate over whether Whitehead is best interpreted as supporting a view of God as one actual occasion or as a serially ordered, "personal" society of actual occasions. If the former, then God would be an exception to the categoreal scheme as an actual entity which does not exist in time. The former interpretation is rejected by Cobb (1965a, 187 ff.) because Whitehead affirms that both the primordial and consequent natures of God have causal efficacy, for example, when Whitehead says that the "perfected actuality [of God] passes back into the temporal world, and qualifies this world so that each temporal actuality includes it as an immediate fact of relevant experience" (1978, 351). In order to "pass back into the temporal world" God would have to be prehended by new occasions. But only an actual entity which has reached satisfaction or completion can be prehended. If God is a single, eternal, actual entity, then God can never reach satisfaction, which would contradict the possibility of God's consequent nature, and thus of the meaning of an actual entity. Therefore, Cobb concludes that God is best interpreted as a living person—"a succession of moments of experience with special continuity" (1965a, 188).

In sum, Cobb conceives God as related to the world through the divine provision of an initial aim. The initial aim consists of an ideal aim along with a set of relevant possibilities "appropriate to the situation although deviating from the ideal" (1965a, 154). From this set of possibilities that make up the initial aim, the occasion derives its subjective aim, that is, derives its own aim toward realization according to which it determines its satisfaction or value. God's prehension of the subsequent actualization of the world passes back into the world to be prehended by the world. In less technical language, God's desire for the world becomes part of the world and thus is in some way—usually unconsciously—a part of our experience.

The initial aim then both limits an actual occasion's freedom in achieving satisfaction by limiting relevant possibilities, yet makes free decision possible by providing a set of realizable possibilities for actualization. Thus, an actual occasion is free to choose whether to actualize the ideal possibilities for its—and God's—fullest satisfaction, or to actualize lesser values (1965a, 154). Ontologically, then, it is possible that a human occasion may completely make the ideal aim its subjective aim; however, ontically this appears to happen only to relative degree (1966, 144). Moreover, it is ontologically possible that the initial aim provided to an occasion of human experience emphasize God's own feeling of the world as its main content (1966, 146). Where this is the case, and where the human occasion makes this its subjective aim, then one can say that God is

incarnate in that individual (1966, 146). Cobb believes this ontological possibility was ontically true of Jesus of Nazareth.

Hence, Cobb understands Jesus as one who prehends God's
presence both in terms of God's ideal aim for him and in terms of
God's consequent nature by which God objectifies the divine aim so
as to play a peculiar role in Jesus' existence. Although all prehension is selective and generally unconscious, it is nonetheless a re-
enactment of another occasion. In Jesus' case, his prehension or re-
enactment of God's presence uniquely and extensively qualified his
consciousness and existence (1965c, 13).

Cobb's understanding of the incarnation has three advantages
for a theology which nurtures faith. First, on the one hand, this view
maintains the divine initiative of the incarnation, for only God can
provide the initial aim that both includes the divine experience and is
relevant to Jesus' experience; on the other hand, this view maintains
Jesus' individual personhood, for Jesus is still understood as deciding,
in each moment of his existence, to make the initial aim of God his
own subjective aim (1966, 146). Second, insofar as individuality and
self-determination are fulfilled by an actual occasion's conformity to
the ideal aim provided by God, one can say that Jesus was most fully
free and fulfilled insofar as he incarnated God (1966, 147). Finally, a
Whiteheadian explanation does not reduce the "mystery" or meaning
of the incarnation to psychological drives or to another form of experience in order to make it accord with empirical knowledge and experience. Rather, it assumes the integrity of the experience of those
who claim that they have experienced God in Jesus Christ, and it tries
to provide an understanding of the experience that is broad enough to
acknowledge the truth of faith and knowledge.

Cobb's understanding of the efficacy of Jesus for the present
day Christian and Cobb's exposition of how the incarnation of God
in Christ is possible illustrate the ability of Whitehead's cosmology
to aid theological method. It clearly is beyond the limits set forth
here to do more than illustrate the potential of Whitehead's thought
to overcome obstacles to faith, because ultimately the adequacy of
any cosmology can be judged only by its comprehensiveness in
dealing with specific issues. However, the overall success of Cobb's
theology provides significant evidence for the general excellence of
Whitehead's cosmology, and thus its potential value for theological
method. Moreover, Whitehead's cosmology is amenable to the in-

tegrity of religious experience; for example, in his understanding of
the occasion's prehension of the ideal aim, Whitehead affirms, like
Cobb, that the experience of God precedes human interpretation of
experience. Finally, even as Cobb draws on Whitehead's notion of
prehension to understand the incarnation, Whitehead himself acknowledges the relationship between prehension and incarnation from
a different direction when he argues that the Christian notion of incarnation points to the "solution of a fundamental metaphysical
problem," namely, the nature of God's relationship to the world, and
is thereby the only fundamental improvement on Plato's metaphysics
(1933, 167 ff.). In short, Cobb finds in Whitehead a philosophy not
only consistent with empirical knowledge, but also congenial to
much in Christian experience.

CONCLUSIONS

EMPIRICAL METHOD IN THEOLOGY

The preceding analysis outlines the central aspects of Cobb's
theological method and points to how his method is related to his
christology. I have shown that in his pre-1969 period, Cobb developed a profound empirical theology that has gone far in its original
blending of empiricist, neo-orthodox, and rationalist insights.
Cobb's method is fundamentally empirical in its principal aim,
namely, to elucidate beliefs so as to be consistent with empirical
knowledge and experience. This aim both defines the problem that
method is to solve and indicates the ultimate criterion by which the
results of method are to be judged. Moreover, Cobb's understanding
of faith as an experience preceding interpretation identifies faith with
other fundamental human experiences which are the bases of knowledge about the world, rather than the result of knowledge or an exception to human experience and knowledge.

Cobb's indebtedness to Wieman's empiricism can be seen in
his conviction that faith is an empirical experience which can be analyzed in empirical terms. However, unlike Wieman, Cobb does not
believe that an empirical description of the experience of faith is sufficient in nurturing that faith, and is thus not sufficient for theological method.

Moreover, Cobb takes seriously Barth's neo-orthodox affirmation that the biblical witness is fundamental to Christian theology—even a Christian natural theology. However, Cobb rejects as
existentially closed the neo-orthodox supposition that this unique
witness can only be understood as a supernatural event that radically
transcends knowledge and experience.

In theory, theological method requires consistency with empirical knowledge and experience; in practice, process philosophy
serves this requirement for Cobb. The resulting, conspicuous role of
process philosophy in Cobb's method shows his indebtedness to
Hartshorne and seems to contribute to Tracy's and Ogden's preference
to drop "Christian" from Christian natural theology. Nevertheless,
Cobb's pre-1969 view of philosophy differs profoundly from that of
Hartshorne, Tracy, and Ogden, in that he believes that even the most
excellent philosophy depends upon the vision of the world that it
presupposes.

In spite of his indebtedness to Wieman, Barth, and
Hartshorne, Cobb parts company with all three over the role of speculation in method. For Cobb, as for Whitehead, speculation is how
we move from immediate experience to knowledge about the world.
Put differently, it is how we move from the particulars of experience
to the generalities of knowledge. It is necessary to knowledge, but it
is dependent upon experience for its origin and for the test of its adequacy. Speculation is thus not only needed in talk about God, it is
needed in formulating scientific theories, for, as Whitehead states in
Process and Reality, pure induction breaks down when we wish to
discover scientific theories or laws:

> This collapse of the method of rigid empiricism . . .
> occurs whenever we seek larger generalities. In natural
> science this rigid method is the Baconian method of
> induction, a method which, if consistently pursued,
> would have left science where it found it. What Bacon
> omitted was the play of a free imagination, controlled
> by the requirements of coherence and logic. The true
> method of discovery is like the flight of an aeroplane.
> It starts from the ground of particular observation; it
> makes a flight in the thin air of imaginative general-
> ization; and it again lands for renewed observation
> rendered acute by rational interpretation. (1978, 4 f.)

Nonetheless, Cobb does recognize the dangers of speculation. This is evident in his understanding of the religious problem to which theological method is to respond. However, he does not resolve the problem of speculation by avoiding it, but rather by responsibly incorporating speculation in theology. Speculation in theological method does not undermine faith if it is recognized as a response to the experience of faith, that is, if it is recognized that speculation is grounded in faith, not faith in speculation. Thus, when beliefs come into conflict with experience and knowledge, reflective Christians are forced neither to deny any relationship between faith and experience and knowledge, nor to reject the grounds of faith or knowledge. This is not to say that neither one's faith or vision of reality nor one's knowledge and experience is exempt from need of revision in the light of each other. Rather, "a person . . . should believe what commends itself to him in its own right. . . . If he remains Christian it is because he finds that Christian faith, properly understood, seems true in light of all that one can learn" (1969c, 95). In this sense, Cobb sees himself fundamentally as an empirical theologian (1969c, 95).

CHRISTOLOGY

Because of the fundamental role that the primitive Christian witness has in Cobb's theology, christology has significance for method in two ways. First, insofar as the primitive witness of Christian faith originates historically in the encounter with Jesus of Nazareth, what can be known historically about Jesus helps the theologian understand this witness better. This is not to say that the primitive witness is a witness about Jesus' history, but it is to acknowledge, as Cobb does, that the witness refers to the change in existence that ensued from early Christians' encounter with a historical person. What is discovered of the historical Jesus then does not determine the primitive witness, but gives insight into the nature of the experience of those who have encountered Jesus so as to be transformed in their existence.

Second, we have noted that insofar as some contemporary Christians directly experience Jesus Christ, the theologian needs to elucidate the meaning of Jesus Christ in light of present knowledge and experience. This is not to say that there are not more fundamental problems for faith which demand the theologian's attention, for certainly the questions of the nature of God and God's relationship to the world are logically more basic. However, the problem of understanding the meaning of Jesus Christ exists so long as people's encounter with him, direct or indirect, is the origin of their structure of existence.

Although christology has a role in Cobb's theology, it would not be accurate to term it a "christocentric" theology as one might Barth's. The Christian vision has historical roots in Jesus Christ, but, according to Cobb, it can and often does exist independently of conscious indebtedness to those roots. Although it is possible for a modern person to experience Christ personally, that experience is not required for a person to have attained the Christian structure of existence (1969a, 11). Hence, Cobb's starting point is a particular kind of human existence that has historical continuity with Jesus Christ. Cobb generally assumes that proper beliefs about Christ can nurture that existence—an existence which is difficult to maintain in a world that encourages self indulgence over self-transcendence—but he also notes that this existence may benefit quite well from intensive therapy of encounter groups (1969a, 11). Thus, although beliefs about Jesus Christ might generally nurture that existence, they do not appear to be directly necessary to initiating that existence in a contemporary person. This view, unlike neo-orthodoxy, ultimately gives minimal importance to christology. Indeed, to the extent that Jesus Christ is peripheral to Christian faith, that is, to the Christian structure of existence, christology is peripheral to theological method.

ETHICAL IMPLICATIONS

Not only is the starting point of theology the Christian structure of existence, insofar as theology is in service of the church, its goal is to further that existence, because the "purpose or mission of the Christian church [is] to be the sustaining, nurturing, and extending of . . . Christian existence" (1969a, 9 f.). This understanding of theology as furthering the Christian structure of existence has important implications for a theological ethics. Specifically, it implies a normative character theory. This character theory de-emphasizes outward behavior and rules and is concerned fundamentally with motivation and intention. Such an ethic is primarily a "matter of the heart." James Gustafson has noted that character theory generally has many negative implications for Christian ethics, associated with an individualistic and self-preoccupied (if not self-centered) morality (1968, 81). Cobb appears to recognize this potential danger with regard to spiritual structure of existence in particular (1967b, 122 f.); but he also notes that *Christian* existence is fulfilled in love, thus it leads to openness to others. Moreover, as we will see in the next chapter with reference to Cobb's anthropology, Gustafson's characterization does not easily follow from a Whiteheadian understanding of the human occasion of experience.

NOTES

1. In *Living Options*, Cobb divides neo-orthodoxy into two types: "theological positivism" and "theological existentialism." Barth is the most radical exponent of the former, which also includes Brunner. Bultmann is the most radical exponent of existentialism, which also includes Tillich and the Niebuhr brothers. Although Cobb presents both Barth and Bultmann as "genuine alternatives" in theological method to his own proposal of Christian natural theology, I have decided to focus only on Barth, both for the sake of brevity and because Cobb sees Barth and Bultmann as living options for basically the same reasons: their radical supernaturalism and monistic view of grace (1962, 320). Cobb's discussion of Bultmann can be found in *Living Options*, chap. 9.

2. In the final chapter (written in 1960) of *God and the World* (1969b) Cobb raises the question, "Is Christian Theology Still Possible?", based upon the observation that the Judeo-Christian vision of the world (viz., experience of the world as creation) appears to be no longer available to modern consciousness (123). On the surface this implies that the theologian would be unable to begin with the Christian vision of reality. In this context, theology must either "justify or preserve" the Judeo-Christian vision or abandon it (124). The latter option Cobb associates with Barth and Bultmann because they describe faith as completely independent of any vision of the cosmos. In *God and the World* Cobb rejects abandonment in favor of re-establishing the Christian vision in the context of modern consciousness. When one keeps in mind that the goal of method is to remove obstacles to faith, one can readily see that preserving or defending the Christian vision is in continuity with that aim.

Moreover, in order for theology to preserve and defend the Christian vision of the world, it must still begin with this vision.

3.   Cobb uses the term "vision of reality" in *Living Options*, *Christian Natural Theology*, and *God and the World* to refer to what he believed to be essential to Christianity. In *God and the World*, Cobb also talks about the Judeo-Christian vision of the world, (viz., the experience of the world as creation), which I take to be a broader vision, inclusive of the Christian vision itself. In a letter, (May 30, 1985), Cobb notes that he switched to the notion of structure of existence because it "probed more deeply into the pre-conscious, pre-interpreted reality," although he continued to think of the structure of existence as closely related to the vision of reality: "A vision of reality both expresses and encourages a structure of existence." For the purpose of this essay, I do not make a sharp distinction between the two, but rather see the structure of Christian existence as a refinement of the Christian vision of reality.

4.   Cobb does not attempt to cite New Testament texts to support his assertions about Jesus and his effect on the early Christian community. This could be construed as a weakness in his analysis, although I believe that it simply reflects both expedience and trust that the work of biblical scholars bears out his generalizations. Without a doubt, Cobb's analysis would benefit from more explicit textual criticism, which is being done in some quarters. For example, one essay that argues that a dipolar view of God follows more appropriately from New Testament study—specifically, in terms of christology—than from a philosophical analysis such as Hartshorne's is Thomas Ogletree's "A Christological Assessment of Dipolar Theism" found in *Process Philosophy and Christian Thought* (Brown, James & Reeves 1971, 331-46).

5.   Cobb makes a distinction between personal existence and prophetic existence, on the one hand, and between spiritual existence and Christian existence, on the other. The use of "personal" or "spiritual" existence leaves open how the structure of existence is "fulfilled" and whether it is expressed in a morally good way. Hence spiritual existence is equally capable of being expressed in invidious self-preoccupation as well as self-transcending love (1967b, 134). The use of "prophetic" and "Christian" refer to the normative, rather than merely formal, aspects of the personal and spiritual existences, respectively. Thus, prophetic existence is not simply ethical consciousness, but ethical consciousness standing in obedience to God the creator; and Christian existence is not simply self-transcending self, but self-transcending self fulfilled in love.

6. Of course, logically, there are some more fundamental problems that arise whenever one talks about human experience of God, in particular what is the nature of a God who participates in concrete events? Much of *A Christian Natural Theology* can be read as a response to that question. I confine myself to the nature of Jesus because of Cobb's assertion that a Christian natural theology assumes as its starting point the Christian vision which historically has grown out of Jesus Christ, and because I will be examining his shift in christology after 1969 and its relationship to ethics.

CHAPTER TWO

ETHICAL THEORY BEFORE 1969

In the previous chapter, I surveyed the basic elements of John Cobb's Christian natural theology, examined some of the implications his method holds for anthropology and christology, and briefly alluded to the significance of these implications for ethics. In this chapter I turn directly to Cobb's early ethical theory. Before 1969, Cobb's first concern in addressing ethical theory is to try to demonstrate that the ground of ethics is independent of theological and cosmological considerations. Hence, Cobb's earliest writings on ethics reflect an interest in formal questions about the nature and ground of ethics. In fact, what is most noticeable in observing the differences between Cobb's ethical writings before 1969 and his writings after 1969 is that the former are concerned primarily with formal or metaethical questions, such as the nature of obligation and value, whereas the latter are concerned with substantive or normative issues, such as ecology, feminism, and economics. It can even be argued that Cobb had little in the line of a social ethics before his concern with ecology. This argument holds insofar as one considers the number of Cobb's publications on social and political issues. It must be qualified, however, both with regard to the social implications of his formal ethical theory and with regard to Cobb's own personal involvement in social issues.[1] Moreover, there is considerable continuity in Cobb's thought, from his dissertation to his interest in political theology. Most conspicuously, Whitehead's philosophy has remained integral to Cobb's theology. Consequently, one would find

it difficult to understand Cobb's later ecological and political prescriptions without first comprehending the philosophical tradition
from which Cobb has always drawn.

Nonetheless, Cobb's earlier preoccupation with the question
of method influenced his early concern with ethics, directing his attention first to metaethical issues. For this reason, it seems fair to
say that there is a trajectory in Cobb's thinking from formal to substantive issues, and perhaps even from personal ethics to social
ethics. This chapter will analyze the central features of Cobb's ethical thought before he turns fully to deal with substantive social issues. In particular, I look at how Cobb's ethics grows out of his interest in theological method. Then I examine Cobb's theories of
obligation, value, and character, arguing—as implied at the end of the
previous chapter—that Cobb's theory of character is central to his
early Christian ethics. In the next chapter, I will argue that Cobb's
eventual turn toward substantive ethical issues brings about a profound shift in his theological method and christology.

THE TASK FOR ETHICAL THEORY

Just as Cobb's early theological method does not start with
Whitehead's cosmology and construct a process theology on that
basis, so too, Cobb's early ethics does not simply presuppose
Whiteheadian cosmology and derive an ethical theory from it.
Instead, Cobb's interest in ethical theory can be traced, in part, to his
interest in finding a suitable grounding for theological method, on the
one hand, and with his concern for countering the claims by logical
empiricists, such as A. J. Ayer, that no ethical statements have
factual or cognitive warrant, on the other. The first concern is
prominent in his dissertation, where, along with cosmological, empirical, and neo-orthodox options, Cobb explores the possibility of
ethical theory as providing a non-speculative ground for theological
method (1953a, 42 ff.). The second concern emerges most clearly in
A Christian Natural Theology where Cobb attempts to supplement a
Whiteheadian theory of value with a theory of obligation that has
cognitive meaning (1965a, 113 ff.). Although Cobb responds to
these two concerns at different times in his early career, he nonetheless attempts to resolve them in a similar manner, namely, by constructing a "universal normative ethic" which is non-speculative and
has factual warrant (cf. 1954).

In his methodological concern to make religious beliefs immune from being undermined by speculation, Cobb also looks to the possibility of grounding theological method in ethical theory because religious belief has been associated with morality as much as it has with metaphysics (1953a, 42). In other words, just as it is worth examining the possibility of grounding theological method in metaphysics, it is worth examining the possibility of grounding theological method in ethics. If it is possible to provide an ethical theory that is both universal and normative, then, in the tradition of Kant, it may be possible to ground Christian doctrines upon it, thus producing beliefs immune from speculation.

The task of constructing a universal, normative ethic is complicated by the claim of certain logical empiricists and analytic philosophers that normative terms such as "ought" and "should" logically do not refer to factual states of affairs, and at best merely express the speaker's subjective preference. Thus, ethical assertions are without meaning insofar as meaning refers ultimately to factual states of affairs. Cobb is willing to accept this "non-cognitivist" claim to a degree, but he argues that the logical status of normative statements does not require one to assume that ethical assertions are not important, and more essentially, it does not require one to assume that ethical assertions are not meaningful or rational, that is, not "uniquely warranted" or justified as correct or incorrect by factual, meaningful statements (1965a, 114). For example, Cobb believes that although a judgment in the form "I ought to do X" is in itself not a verifiable proposition, it may nevertheless be shown to be a correct or incorrect judgment because of its necessary relationship to a verifiable proposition.

TOWARD A UNIVERSAL NORMATIVE ETHIC

Cobb assumes, in a manner reminiscent of Hume, that the feeling or sense of obligation is an "ultimate and irreducible" human experience which is expressed by such terms as "ought" and "should" (1953a, 44; 1965a, 114). Moreover, Cobb assumes that, among the complex of desires, interests, and feelings of obligation which comprise the overall motivation by which a person makes choices, there is "a peculiar and distinct universal human feeling of *moral* obligation" (1954, 56, italics added). Cobb believes that the assumption that there is a uniquely moral sense of obligation is supported by common language, which "bears witness to the presence of such a distinct quality of feeling" (1954, 56). Given this presupposition, Cobb believes we can determine the basis of a universal normative ethic if we can discover some principle to which the feeling of moral obligation universally attaches.

If, when the sense of moral obligation conflicts with the complex of motives of which it is a part, the sense of moral obligation were always modified in favor of that complex, then the sense of moral obligation would be determined entirely by what is desired at the moment. Thus, we would not be able to determine whether our choices were ever made on the basis of our sense of moral obligation, and there would be no possibility of finding a universal normative moral principle implied by the feeling of obligation. However, Cobb notes, if "there is some point at which the feeling of moral obligation necessarily and universally remains independent of the greatest value as determined by the other elements in motivation, then a principle can be formulated such as to point to that behavior which is inescapably felt to be morally right" (1954, 57).

Cobb also assumes, unlike Hume, that free choice extends to ends as well as means. This is an important assumption because if the objects or ends of the total motivation cannot be chosen, then all moral choices are reduced to choices of skill, that is, choices of the best means to pre-given ends (1953a, 47 f.). Cobb defends this assumption by appeal to cultural relativity which has demonstrated that values which are commonly assumed to be ultimate by one culture are unimportant or even disvalued by another. For example, in one culture, liberty and self-interest may be assumed to be ultimate values serving personal fulfillment; whereas in another culture, civic duty and national interest may be assumed to be the ultimate values serving class or racial fulfillment. As a consequence of such knowledge, persons sometimes choose values at odds with those traditionally associated with their cultures.

Usually, such choices of general ends are made for "the greatest satisfaction of the total motivation" according to all knowledge and experience available to a person (1954, 58). But there seem to be occasions in human experience when relevant knowledge and experience threaten one's underlying desires and values. It is here that a universal normative principle can be discerned:

> At some point one may know that if he permitted
> himself to think more clearly on some subject, to be-
> come more intimately acquainted with some person, or
> to immerse himself more deeply in some situation, he
> would be led to desire that [end] which he now abhors.
> This realization may lead him to avoid and to ignore
> this knowledge as far as he can. He may act in accor-
> dance only with that knowledge which does not
> threaten his basic motives, still recognizing that he is
> intentionally ignoring matters of relevance to his de-
> cision. He cannot in this situation escape the attach-
> ment of the feeling of moral obligatoriness to that
> action which would be in accordance with a wider ac-
> ceptance of relevant facts. (1953a, 51)

Unfortunately, Cobb does not give a specific example to illustrate this observation. However, because this observation points
to the universal normative moral principle which Cobb seeks to discover, it is important to examine an example that seems to illustrate
Cobb's observation so as to clarify the relationship between the
feelings of obligation, desire, and interests which comprise one's
overall complex of motivation, on the one hand, and the feelings of
moral obligation, on the other. Hence, I will analyze an interpretation of the way that the character Tevye from the play *Fiddler on
the Roof* deals with two similar moral dilemmas.

Tevye is a poor Jewish peasant in late-19th/early-20th century Russia. On the surface, his overall motivation and desire is to
preserve his "tradition" in the face of a rapidly changing Russia, and,
more specifically, to maintain his Jewish culture and to provide his
family with as prosperous a life as he can. However, the fact that
Tevye actually knows little about his tradition—illustrated by his
frequent attributions of folk wisdom to Torah—indicates that underlying his loyalty to tradition is essentially a fear of the changes
around him that are beyond his control.

In line with his overall motivation, Tevye has the local
matchmaker arrange a marriage for his oldest daughter, Tzeitel, with a
recently widowed and fairly well-to-do butcher. When Tzeitel finds
out, she and the man she loves, a poor tailor, tell Tevye that they
want to talk with him about getting married. At first, Tevye does
not even want to consider his daughter's request because it not only
calls into question the tradition of the father arranging his daughter's

wedding as well as his own desire to see Tzeitel married into a prosperous home, it also threatens his ability to have some control over
this new stage of his family's life. But Tevye recognizes that there
may be other knowledge and experience relevant to the situation and
decides to talk with his daughter and the tailor. In particular, he dis-
covers that his daughter will not be happy with the aging butcher, in
spite of his wealth; and he comes to know and respect the integrity of
the tailor who obviously loves his daughter very much. Although
Tevye is tempted to reject these considerations because they threaten
his overall motivation, he decides nonetheless that he *ought* to take
these other factors into account. This leads him to modify his loyalty to tradition, even at the expense of going back on his word with
the matchmaker and the butcher, although through various manipu-
lations, he keeps some semblance of having the final say in the
matter.

However, when another daughter, Chava, later asks Tevye to
give his blessing to her engagement to a gentile, Tevye flatly refuses
to consider the issue. Chava asks her father simply to meet the person and get to know him before Tevye makes a final decision.
Although Tevye wavers, he decides not to get to know him and ban-
ishes Chava and her fiancé from communication with the rest of his
family. Tevye is not only afraid that if he got to know the fiancé, he
might feel compelled to accept something which he presently detests,
namely, accepting a gentile into his family; he is also fundamentally
afraid to have no real control over such a drastic change in his family's life. Although Tevye's present knowledge and experience—expressed in the form of rationalizations—seem to support his refusal
to meet Chava's fiancé, they do not suffice to remove his feeling of
guilt for his decision not to consider at least getting to know Chava's
fiancé. In Cobb's terms, Tevye's guilt indicates an inescapable tension between his sense that he ought to consider other relevant
knowledge and experience, on the one hand, and his deepest complex
of motives, on the other.

According to this interpretation of the play, in both situations Tevye feels an inescapable obligation to consider relevant
knowledge and experience, namely, to consider what would make his
daughters happy and to get to know their boyfriends better. His refusal to do so in the second situation does not remove the sense of
obligation to consider the relevant facts. In fact, Tevye's refusal illustrates the moral agent's freedom to choose against her or his

feeling of moral obligation. Moreover, Tevye's unsuccessful attempt at rationalizing his refusal indicates the inescapable nature of the obligation, because the tension between the overall complex of motivation and the feeling of moral obligation can only be relieved if the overall motivation is brought into harmony with moral obligation. In other situations where the sense of obligation is not genuinely moral, recognition of the grounds of the feeling of obligation will lead to its eventual removal (1954, 59). (This is illustrated in psychological counseling: when people discover that certain forms of guilt are rooted in a childhood trauma rather than an actual moral feeling, their sense of guilt begins to dissipate.) Finally, it is important to note in this example that the feeling of obligation inescapably attaches first to consideration of relevant knowledge and experience, and only secondarily to the particular course of action recommended by such consideration.

The moral principle revealed in this experience of conflict between the overall complex of motivation and the sense of moral obligation is formulated by Cobb thus: "In any situation that behavior is morally right to which full recognition of all available relevant knowledge and experience would lead the individual involved in that situation" (1954, 59). Cobb notes that this is a definition of what is relatively right, that is, the rightness of an act is relative to one's belief about what is relevant in the given situation. The perfectly right or ideally right would be that behavior which would follow upon perfect knowledge (1954, 59). Cobb appears to recognize that this formulation of the moral principle is too general and in need of refinement, hence, in *A Christian Natural Theology*, he further delineates and expands this principle into what are actually four related principles, each representing a level of development in one's moral experience.

First, of course, one recognizes that one ought to give full consideration to whatever available knowledge and experience appears to one to be relevant (1965a, 119). Second, since intellectual and emotional development affect one's growth in applying this principle, and since "impartial" or "disinterested" reflection represents growth in rationality, one comes to recognize that in moral decisions one ought to view relevant data impartially or disinterestedly (1965a, 120). Third, as one matures, one recognizes that as a morally developed person, one ought to act according to one's duty as that ap-

pears to one upon full, disinterested consideration of relevant knowledge and experience (1965a, 121).

However, disinterested consideration of all relevant factors
generally leads to a tension between attachment of one's sense of
obligation to those acts which will increase intrinsic value and attachment to those acts which are "appropriate to the past," for example, keeping promises (1965a, 122 f.). Put differently, when
making moral decisions, there appear to be two general relevant factors: (a) the value produced by the act and (b) past agreements
(implicit and explicit) that we have made with others. Cobb does not
believe that the tension between these two types of relevant factors is
resolved by subsuming one under the other. For example, one could
argue, in a utilitarian manner, that the reason why keeping promises
is right is because keeping promises generally leads to valuable consequences. Cobb notes, however, that subsuming promise-keeping
under increasing future value would lead one to the absurd conclusion
that one is "ethically bound" to break a promise if doing so would
merely lead to a slight overall increase in value; whereas, "the
keeping of [a] promise has *some* intrinsic rightness independent of
anticipated consequences, and this view seems to be sustained and
strengthened by critical reflection" (1986b, 13).[2] Cobb asserts that
the tension between these two types of obligation calls for some res-
olution, which he finds in a modified version of Kant's principle of
universalizability, namely, "we should so act that we can will that
the maxim by which we act become a universal rule" (1965a, 123).

For Cobb, Kant's principle is an extension of the principle of
disinterestedness to the rules of action which we consider applicable
to a given situation. Cobb notes that Kant argues that the principle
of universalizability is essentially formal—an act cannot be based
upon a maxim which, when willed, leads to self-contradiction when it
is universalized. Cobb, for his part, believes that the principle of
universalizability can apply equally to the consequences which are
likely to follow from our act—an act is wrong when "we may be unable to will that this maxim be followed by all because such action
would lead to consequences we cannot approve" (1965a, 123). Hence,
Cobb incorporates the principle of universalizability into his preceding moral principles to form a fourth moral principle: 'A morally
mature person ought to act in that way in which one would will, on
full consideration of all relevant factors, that all persons should act,
given just these relevant factors' (1965a, 124).

With these principles, Cobb believes he has answered the non-cognitivist objection to normative judgments. Many non-cognitivists readily admit that "ought" may refer to an empirical feeling of obligation, but they argue that all that can be meant by statements such as, "One ought to do X," is either (a) that the speaker merely has a feeling of obligation with reference to X, and thus the statement is a report of the subjective emotions of the speaker; or (b) that the speaker is exhorting others to do X, and thus the statement is an attempt to evoke certain feelings and actions from the hearer. Thus, in both these instances, "One ought to do X," can only be judged as true or false by empirically verifying whether the speaker has a certain feeling or is exhorting others to act in a certain way. The statement is meaningless, non-cognitivists argue, if it is intended to go beyond these instances by expressing a normative judgment—that is, a judgment that the prescription recommended is correct or incorrect—because normative judgments cannot be warranted by empirical judgments (cf. Ayer 1952, 102 ff.).

Cobb's counter-argument is that in at least one other instance, "ought" may also refer to a universal, inescapable sense of obligation. Hence, if "ought" equals a universal, inescapable sense of obligation; and if there is an action (X) toward which all persons have a universal, inescapable sense of obligation; then, "one ought to do X" is both normative and capable of being judged as true or false by verifying that there is an action (X) toward which all persons have a universal, inescapable sense of obligation.

If Cobb's empirical analysis of moral experience is correct, then the first normative principle, 'One ought to give full consideration to whatever available knowledge and experience appears to one to be relevant,' is warranted by the factual statement, 'When one makes a decision, one's sense of obligation is inescapably attached to oneself giving full consideration to whatever knowledge and experience appear relevant' (1965a, 119).[3] Similarly, the second normative principle, 'One ought to view relevant data "impartially" or "disinterestedly",' is warranted by the factual statement, 'One's intellectual and emotional growth lead one to consider data impartially or disinterestedly' (1965a, 120). The third normative principle, 'As a morally developed person, one ought to act according to one's duty as that appears upon full disinterested consideration,' is warranted by the verifiable statement, 'In a morally developed person, the sense of obligation is inescapably attached to the possibility of one acting as one inescapably sees one ought to act on full disinterested consideration of all available knowledge and experience which appear to one to be relevant' (1965a, 121). And finally, the fourth normative principle, 'A morally mature person ought to act in that way in which one would will, on full consideration of all relevant factors, that all persons should act, given just these relevant factors,' is warranted by the statement, 'In a morally developed person, the sense of obligation is inescapably attached to the possibility of one acting as one would will everyone to act upon consideration of all available knowledge and experience which appear to be relevant' (1965a, 124).

I believe that Cobb's overall analysis of moral experience thus far is empirically substantiated, and that he has offered a significant rebuttal to Ayer's type of non-cognitivism. However, I believe it is important to note the fundamental role that the concept "relevant knowledge and experience" plays in Cobb's argument. Once it is acknowledged that relevant knowledge and experience play a role in free choice, then it must be admitted that such knowledge and experience should be considered, for "relevant knowledge and experience" simply mean knowledge and experience that should be considered. Alasdair MacIntyre calls such notions "functional concepts," that is, concepts "defined in terms of the purpose or function which [they] are characteristically expected to serve" (1981, 55). For example, "watch" is always defined with reference to the function of keeping accurate time. If one notes that one's watch does not keep accurate time, it can validly be concluded that it is a bad watch, that is, that it ought to keep better time (1981, 55). Similarly, "relevant knowledge and experience" cannot be defined apart from its being considered by one to whom it is relevant. Thus, if we note that a person does not consider that which she or he knows is relevant knowledge and experience, we can validly conclude that the person is doing something bad, that is, that the person ought to consider the relevant knowledge and experience. By thus including the functional notion of relevant knowledge and experience in his empirical analysis of the sense of obligation, Cobb is able to find factual warrants for normative principles.

Nevertheless, the very notion which makes it possible to provide an empirical warrant for Cobb's universal, normative ethic also makes that ethic too general or formal either to give concrete moral guidance or to provide a grounding for religious beliefs (1953a, 53). For what constitutes relevant knowledge and experience for an agent could mean very little, or almost everything. For example, if one ought to consider what seems to one to be relevant knowledge, then for one who recognizes the complexity of even simple decisions, such as whether one ought to give money to a skid row transient, this might mean that one always ought to seek further knowledge, such as how the transient is likely to use the money, other ways the money could be used, the reasons why this person is a transient, the social impact of transients, and so on ad infinitum. In extreme cases, the attempt to consider all relevant knowledge and experience could lead to an inability to come to a final decision or lead to excessive scrupulosity.

Nonetheless, Cobb's ethics does provide some basic "criteria by which competing definitions of the content of the good can be intelligibly judged in terms of their relevance to the existential human problem of making free choices and decisions" (1953a, 53). If, then, there is some particular knowledge and/or experience which is universally relevant to all moral choices, then Cobb may be able to give more substance to his ethical theory as well as to provide a basis for religious belief. Cobb examines three types of knowledge which might meet the criteria: (a) moral knowledge; (b) knowledge of the self's deepest interests and desires; and (c) knowledge of the events and entities affected by moral choices (1953a, 54).

Universally relevant moral knowledge would be in the form of a universal normative principle or universal, non-speculative understanding of the good. But it was lack of just this sort of knowledge which occasioned Cobb's formulation of an ethical theory. Thus, without resorting to cosmology, there is no hope for further relevant knowledge or experience from this area (1953a, 54).

Universally relevant knowledge of the self's deepest interests and desires seems an impossible ideal in light of the limitations of empirical knowledge and conflicting theories of human motivation. It seems undeniable that some persons are motivated by self-interest, some by pleasure, some by contributing to fullness of life in general, and so on. Since none of these theories has successfully subsumed all the others, such knowledge appears speculative (1953a, 54-56).

Finally, knowledge of the realities universally affected by moral choices would take the form of knowledge of "some reality, itself a constant, affected by all actions and such that for virtually all persons knowledge of it would lead to a feeling such as to uniquely determine action" (1953a, 57). But to ask whether there exists such a reality and what its nature is clearly throws us back upon religious belief and/or cosmological speculation. The only other way that value theory can ground beliefs is if moral experience is interpreted as a direct experience of God. But that leads us back to Wieman's approach to theology, which Cobb has demonstrated does not escape need for cosmological speculation.

Thus, even though Cobb grounds his universal normative ethic independently of theological or cosmological considerations, the formal character of a universal normative ethic disqualifies it from providing a grounding for religious beliefs. In fact, to provide concrete guidelines for moral decisions, his ethic requires cosmological and/or religious beliefs to determine what is relevant to a given decision (1953a, 61). Just as interpretation of religious experience requires cosmology in order to be relevant to the whole of experience, so too interpretation of moral experience requires religious beliefs and/or cosmology to become relevant for concrete situations. Hence, although the formal principles of ethics are autonomous, for Cobb, a comprehensive, practical ethical theory is ultimately not independent of theological and cosmological considerations. For, insofar as ethical theory relies upon religious beliefs and/or cosmology to be concretely relevant, it depends upon some vision of the world. For Cobb then, concrete ethics depends upon a Christian vision of the world and a Christian natural theology to which that experience gives rise.

THEOLOGICAL ETHICS

Although Cobb admits that the integration of ethics with theology is incomplete in much of his pre-1969 work, especially in *A Christian Natural Theology* (letter, 20 July, 1985), the Whiteheadian interpretation that is applied to both human responsibility and the nature of God implies the key features of such an integration. That is, because Cobb's choice of cosmology seeks to give a coherent account of all experience, not just religious experience, it follows that a cosmological account that elucidates both moral and religious experience will provide the superstructure for integrating ethics and theology. Moreover, Cobb's choice of cosmology depends fundamentally upon his basic vision of the world, namely, a Christian vision of the world. Thus, his developed ethics is best understood in light of a Christian natural theology which gives expression to the Christian vision of the world.

As the previous section indicates, Cobb's formal ethical theory grows out of his analysis of the nature of obligation. In working out his concrete ethics, Cobb is concerned with exploring two other fundamental notions traditional to ethical theory, namely, the nature of value and its relationship to obligation, and the nature of human existence and its implications for character theory.[4] In the analysis below, I look at how Cobb works out his theory of value in light of his Whiteheadian cosmology and his understanding of the nature of God, as well as how Cobb comprehends the relationship of value to obligation. Then I examine the ethical implications of his anthropology in *A Christian Natural Theology*, touching briefly upon its relationship to the Christian structure of existence discussed in chapter one.

THEORY OF VALUE

In the tradition of ethicists like William Frankena who notes that "we cannot or should not determine what is morally right or wrong without considering whether what we do or propose to do will have good or evil results" (1973, 79 f.), Cobb states that "right conduct must be directed toward the realization of high values" (1965a, 108). Hence, Cobb offers a cosmological analysis of the nature of value so as to shed some light upon what is relevant to our moral decisions.

The basic notion in any value theory is that of intrinsic value, that is, that which is valued for its own sake as an end in itself, not for what it produces. Cobb follows Whitehead in the conviction that the locus of intrinsic value is the actual occasion. He rejects attributing value to qualities because qualities are nonexistent in abstraction from actual entities (1965a, 98). Thus, the only type of thing that can be valuable is an actual occasion or an event, that is, a determinate nexus of actual occasions (1965a, 98-100). But the determinate unity of a nexus is either formal, and thus an abstraction from existence, or it is objectified by an actual occasion, and thus only has unity in the prehension of a single occasion. Therefore, the locus of value lies ultimately in individual actual occasions. Moreover, intrinsic value must lie in the subjective immediacy of individual occasions—that is, in concrescing occasions rather than in completed occasions—because when subjective immediacy passes, the occasion perishes and "becomes an influence upon the future and has value for that future, but it is no longer a value in itself" (1965a, 100). In other words, intrinsic value refers to a present actual occasion's intensity of feeling, whereas instrumental value refers to the feeling that past actual occasions contribute to present occasions.

Although the locus of value is in the individual actual occasion, the possibility of experiencing value derives from God's relationship to the world. Again drawing upon Whitehead, Cobb notes that it is God who makes achievement of value possible by primordially operating as a principle of limitation or concretion, that is, by providing to each occasion a scaled set of possibilities or eternal objects through which new intensities of feeling can be achieved (1965a, 156). God provides this scaled set of eternal objects through an initial aim toward final synthesis, hence directing the occasion, relevant to its established past, toward "the greatest intensity of feeling and also [toward contributing] maximally to the future nexus of which it is a part" (1965a, 154). As was noted in the previous chapter, Cobb goes beyond Whitehead's view that the initial aim derives solely from God's primordial nature by pointing to the role of God's consequent nature in making the initial aim relevant to the occasion. Specifically, Cobb points out that God's own concrescence (i.e., achievement of value), in accord with God's own aim toward value, is self-constituted in such a way as to influence the future occasion with an appetition toward achieving ideal value within the relevant context of the occasion (i.e., the context provided by the occasion's past, which includes God).

Cobb's view that the initial aim toward value derives from the dipolar nature of God as making primordial possibilities relevant through God's own experience of value, not only means that the intrinsic value of each actual occasion comes from God, but that, in turn, each occasion's achievement of value contributes to God's (and therefore all occasions') subsequent experience. In fact, God's own achievement of value is the most concrete, the most inclusive, and the most profound, because God most fully incorporates the feeling or prehension of all concrete actuality into the divine experience. This means, in turn, that God's concrescence aims at the greatest value for all occasions, for insofar as each occasion achieves greater fullness of experience or being, God achieves greater fullness of being (1965a, 180).

The locus of value then is the subjective immediacy of each individual occasion, including God, and the possibility of achieving value arises in the dynamic relationship between the concrescence of God and the concrescence of all other actual occasions. But the question remains as to what the nature of value or intensity of feeling is. The equation of value with intensity of feeling appears to point to some type of hedonism—an interpretation that seems, on the surface, to be supported by Whitehead's description of the aim toward intensity of feeling as an "aim toward satisfaction." However, Cobb rejects this interpretation of the experience of value because in human experience we often prefer painful, complex, rich experiences over the pleasureful, simple, trivial experiences. Ironically borrowing from John Stuart Mill's version of hedonism to illustrate his point, Cobb notes that "many of us would prefer to share with Socrates an experience of pain than to share with a pig the experience of contentment" (1965a, 101). Cobb follows Whitehead in referring to this aim toward intensity of feeling as the aim toward "strength of beauty."

Why do Cobb and Whitehead turn to an aesthetic category to describe the nature of value? Beauty generally refers to "a certain harmony of proportions and relations" (1965a, 101). The concrescence of an actual occasion is its synthesis of its prehensions of past occasions and of relevant eternal objects in accord with its subjective aim. These prehensions are the elements of experience—the experience is the actual occasion or concrescence itself. The final synthesis is a harmonization of these elements into a new experience, that is, it is an achievement of a new feeling or value. Hence, because the new feeling or value is determined by the harmony of proportions and relations of the prehensions constituting the concrescence, Whitehead and Cobb find it appropriate to term it an achievement of beauty. "Beauty" then does not necessarily refer to sense experience (1965a, 102), nor directly to a quality belonging to things experienced (1965a, 101); rather, it refers to the harmony of proportions and relations of the total experience of an occasion.

Cobb considers discord—that which threatens the possibility of achieving harmony, and thus beauty—to be the fundamental evil. Discord occurs when there are mutually inhibiting elements in an occasion's synthesis of prehensions. Because discord involves the presence of mutually exclusive elements, rather than say "an absence of being," Cobb calls discordant feeling a "positive" and "intrinsic" evil, "and to the extent that it is predominant, we may speak of the occasion as a negative value" (1965a, 102).

It should be noted that at this stage of his thinking Cobb does not appear to carry out the analysis of evil quite as far as Whitehead. Although Whitehead acknowledges that discord "is the feeling of evil in the most general sense" (1933, 256), he also points out that "the ultimate evil in the temporal world . . . lies in the fact that the past fades, that time is a 'perpetual perishing'" (1978, 340). But in his early writings, Cobb focuses only upon the notion of discord and does not relate the notion of perpetual perishing to evil. Indeed, in some of these writings the question of perishing, or for human occasions, the question of death, "does not seem [to Cobb] especially evil" (1967, 4). Certainly for Whitehead the evil of discord is that it contributes to elimination of obstructive elements (1978, 340), but in itself it is not intrinsically evil. And in fact, discord is sometimes the occasion for advance in value: "The contribution to Beauty which can be supplied by Discord—in itself destructive and evil—is the positive feeling of a quick shift of aim from the tameness of outworn perfection to some other ideal with its freshness still upon it" (1933, 257). On this latter point, Cobb is in agreement with Whitehead, namely, that discord can sometimes be integrated into a richer harmony and thus become an opportunity for new achievement of beauty, analogous to the way a composer can weave a discordant melody into a larger composition where it contributes to a greater beauty.

One reason why discord, although it can destroy harmony, does not necessarily destroy beauty is because simple harmony is not the sole criterion of beauty. Harmony can be completely free of discord and yet trivial if it lacks "strength of beauty." In other words, although some minimum harmony must necessarily be present for an experience to achieve beauty, "strength of beauty" requires complexity (or qualitative variety) and intensity (or quantity) among the elements of the experience (1965a, 103). Hence, there is a vast difference between the trivial, though possibly pervasive harmony experienced by the dominant occasion of a contented pig, and the complex and intense, though possibly tenuous harmony experienced by the dominant occasion of a neurotic human being. Even though the experience making up a contented pig may be more harmonious than that of a neurotic human, the experience of a human is more beautiful because of the complexity and magnitude of its synthesis. Thus, the measure of beauty depends upon the harmony and strength of an experience, that is, upon the harmony of the complexity and magnitude of its elements: "An experience of great strength is certainly preferable to a trivial one even if it is considerably less harmonious. On the other hand, a slight gain in strength may not counterbalance a loss of harmony, and great strength accompanied by serious discord may be inferior to a simple and placid harmony. . . . [H]ence no single scale for the evaluation of beauty is possible" (1965a, 103).

The difficulty in evaluating beauty leads to "a plurality of relevant ideals [of value] that may be legitimately espoused" (1965a, 104). For example, there is likely to be disagreement between those who seek simple, but safe harmonies and those who are willing to risk discord to attain richer complexities (1965a, 104). Hence, cultural relativity can be understood in terms of societies seeking, on the whole, equally valid ideals of beauty. Nevertheless, although the measure of value is complex and individual, and although cultural ideals of beauty are relative, there is a single ideal of beauty that offers an ultimate perspective for evaluation. This ideal is "maximum strength of beauty," that is, the harmonious balance of maximum massiveness and maximum intensity (1965a, 103 f.). This ideal is also God's eternally unchanging aim for the world and for God's own experience (1965a, 180 f.).

However, simply to pursue attainment of the maximum beauty *immediately available* is not necessarily consistent with right action because such pursuit can lead to "endless repetitions [of an experience] that lose their intensity" rather than to "the realization of high values" (1965a, 108). As noted above, God provides each individual occasion with an initial aim toward beauty that is relevant—thus relative—to its situation. However, each occasion determines for itself, in light of its causal past and the initial aim, its subjective aim toward value. The occasion's subjective aim can easily be directed merely to repeating previous achievements of beauty or avoiding discord, and hence there is often the tendency to seek trivial harmonies of feeling rather than a new ideal beauty (1965a. 102 f., 108). Mere elimination of discord or repetition of past attainment of beauty lessens the intensity of feeling so that the intrinsic value of the occasion of experience becomes trivial. This tendency toward triviality describes the cosmological basis of such experiences as alcohol or drug addiction. Not surprisingly, Whitehead notes the temptation of substituting the aim toward "anaesthesia" for the aim toward beauty (see 1933, 256, 259, 263).

Although neither Whitehead nor, to my knowledge, Cobb refers to triviality as a positive evil—Whitehead, in fact, is careful to note that triviality does not take away from attained beauty (1933, 256)—they both point out that triviality is the greatest threat to the achievement of new value. Discord or positive evil can lead to decay, but it can also be taken up into greater harmonies and thus become an opportunity for greater achievements of value. Conversely, to achieve greater values, one must risk discord. Thus, discord is the necessary risk to growth in value. Triviality, on the other hand, is rejection of new possibilities, and thus rejection of attainment of future value. Moreover, because "the effect of the present on the future is the business of morals" (Whitehead 1933, 269), triviality appears to be at the heart of moral evil, because its tendency to repeat attained value prevents sacrifice of present attainment of beauty "for the sake of a greater beauty to be attained in the future" (Cobb 1965a, 108 f.; cf. Whitehead 1933, 269).

Morality, then, refers to what is necessary to bring about greater value in the future and to avoid relapse into triviality and decay (Whitehead 1933, 269). Put differently, morality is concerned with achieving an ideal balance or synthesis between present attainment of value and future attainment of value, while emphasizing "taking into account the larger rather than the more limited future" (Cobb 1965a, 111). To say that morality has to do with the attainment of future values is to say that morality has to do with contributing to the value of others, because the future of an occasion, by definition, refers to all other subsequent occasions. In one sense there is a moral dimension to every occasion because each occasion aims at some intensity of feeling for its relevant future (1965a, 109). Although the relevant future of an occasion primarily includes those occasions which have personal identity with it, the relationship, say, "of my present occasion of experience to the future occasions of my experience is not entirely unlike its relation to future occasions of other persons such as my child" (1965a, 110). For this reason, Cobb finds the self-interest theory of ethics metaphysically implausible (1965a, 110).

It is important to note at this point that, although Cobb construes the nature of intrinsic value as beauty, he believes that beauty is transcended—though not set aside—by the value of peace (1965a, 131). Beauty, by its nature can be superseded from moment to moment; that is, there is always open to the future the possibility of an increase in the richness and intensity of experience. However, the possibility for increase in beauty also indicates that beauty is transient—"beauty fades," perhaps to be lost forever and never superseded (1965a, 131). In part, the fact that beauty must fade is one reason why moral value is important, for moral value is concerned with the future increase of beauty. Cobb points out, however, that the quest for new value may itself be experienced as meaningless because it cannot guarantee the triumph of beauty over triviality and discord (1965a , 131 f.). Hence, if beauty "is to be enjoyed without the poignant doubt of its worth, there must be an intuition that the worth of beauty exceeds its momentary enjoyment, that its attainment is self-justifying beyond the ability of reason to grasp its value" (1965a, 132). This means that the intrinsic value experienced in beauty is itself undergirded by a more profound experience of the ultimate worth of all experience. This "Harmony of Harmonies" is experienced as a gift and "is not a function of particular cognitive beliefs more or less intensely held; it is a direct apprehension of one's relatedness with that factor in the universe which is divine" (1965a, 133).

Cobb readily admits that at this point in Whitehead's philosophy, we are "on the threshold of religion, or more accurately, well across the threshold" (1965a, 133), and identifies peace with "the vision of God," that is faith in an ultimate reality which preserves and redeems the worth of all experience (1965a, 221-23). Hence, Cobb's most profound speculations presuppose an existential apprehension of the ultimate value of existence. In this way, Cobb comes full circle and implicitly identifies the underlying confidence in the meaningfulness and worth of beauty and morality with the starting point for Christian natural theology, namely, the Christian vision of reality.

Cobb's analysis of value raises two further questions for our understanding of his moral theory: (a) Beyond Cobb's basic assumption that value is a relevant factor in making moral decisions, what is the cosmological basis of the relationship between obligation and value? and (b) Has Cobb moved beyond a merely formal ethics?

As we have seen, every occasion of experience aims at value inasmuch as it aims at satisfaction. God makes the achievement of value possible by providing each occasion with an initial, ideal aim toward beauty. This "initial aim is felt as a proposition whose logical subject is the occasion and whose predicate is the ideal possibility for realization, that is, the ideal harmony possible for that occasion. It is an aim at a balance between the intensity of that occasion's experience and its contribution beyond itself" (1965a., 128). Hence, for each occasion, God aims at the greatest realization of value which at the same time increases the possibility of achieving new value for future occasions. Elsewhere, Cobb has called this activity of God in the satisfaction of the occasion the "call forward" which "calls us so to actualize ourselves in that moment as to embody some ideal maximum of experience which is at the same time compatible with the realization of values by other occasions of experience in our own future and in the wider world" (1969b, 54 f.). Each occasion prehends this ideal aim or "call" and determines for itself a subjective aim at value that will always partly conform to the ideal aim. In short, each occasion prehends the ideal achievement of value available to it but determines for itself its final actualization.

An entity's prehension of a past occasion is accompanied by an emotional tone or *subjective form* that conforms in part to the subjective form of that which is prehended (1965a, 34). The subjective form refers to *how* something is prehended rather than what is prehended. Whitehead suggests there are several species of subjective forms, including "emotions, valuations, purposes, adversions, aversions, consciousness, etc." (1978, 24). The sense of obligation is one species of subjective form. Specifically, the sense of obligation is the subjective form of the prehension of a proposition of which the occasion is the logical subject, and a possible mode of behavior is the predicate (1965a, 114 f.; 1964, 214). As I noted above, the ideal aim is such a proposition, and is thus accompanied by the subjective form of obligation. Put differently, an occasion's prehension of God's ideal aim for it is accompanied by the "subjective form of appetition conformal to that of God"; that is, its "subjective form . . . include[s] desire for realization" (1965a, 153, 183).

The subjective form of obligation can accompany many prehensions other than the ideal aim, but *moral* obligation only accompanies the prehension of the ideal aim. This follows from the understanding of morality as concerned with the ideal synthesis between present and future value, because the prehension of the ideal aim is the only prehension that takes into account the ideal balance between present attainment of value and contribution to future value for a given situation. Moreover, prehension of the ideal aim clearly corresponds to the ideally right as defined above in Cobb's universal normative ethic. That is, prehension of the ideal aim is prehension of that possible behavior which would follow upon perfect knowledge, for God's ideal aim for the occasion follows upon perfect knowledge. In prehending the ideal aim at value, one also experiences a subjective form of obligation to actualize that ideal. Hence, the source of the feeling of moral obligation coincides with the source of the ideal aim at value.

We have seen that the feeling of moral obligation categorically attaches to the moral principles outlined in Cobb's universal, normative ethic. These universal normative principles provide a rational method for calculating which of the possible actions or rules is right for the agent. Moreover, they point to what is ideally right, namely that which is deemed right after consideration of all relevant knowledge and experience, which, we have seen, coincides with the ideal aim at value. Paradoxically, the "strenuous effort" required to approximate what is ideally right by considering all relevant knowledge and being consistently impartial can result in "a certain rigidity, insensitivity, and pride that militate against the achievement of beauty both in oneself and others" (1965a, 125). To avoid this paradoxical result, Cobb asserts that there must be a possibility of transcending ethical duty proper—narrowly conceived as rational calculation of what is right—by becoming directly responsive to the ideal aim at value.[5]

Cobb identifies direct responsiveness to the ideal aim as sensitivity to or trust in "conscience" (1965a, 129 f.). Although Cobb does not explain in much detail the experience of this openness to the ideal aim, he does note that it is similar to what we commonly call "conscience, intuition, or instinct," but that it is not the same as fear of consequences, or superego, or whim, or animal reflex. Rather, an occasion's experience of the ideal aim is an experience of something that comes from beyond itself, "that new thing which in conjunction with the whole force of the past initiates the process in which a new occasion comes to be" (1965a, 129). Hence, the experience of moral conscience is marked by a sense of transcendence and novelty, the achievement of new value.

I believe Cobb's cursory description can be supplemented by referring back to his discussion of the sense of moral obligation. The subjective form of moral obligation always accompanies the ideal aim. Therefore, each individual occasion experiences a moral obligation to enact the ideal aim. Cobb's universal normative ethic can be understood as an attempt to demonstrate that consideration of all relevant knowledge and experience is universally prescribed by the ideal aim, and thus, that the sense of obligation attaching to such consideration is universally moral.

However, the ideal aim is always relative to the individual occasion; that is, it always aims at the ideal achievable in the given context of the occasion. Thus, there are specific prescriptions contained in the ideal aim, which, of course, are accompanied by specific subjective forms of moral obligation. An individual often experiences these subjective forms of moral obligation unconsciously, mixed with other types of subjective forms, such as emotions and purposes. The proliferation of subjective forms makes it difficult for the individual occasion to discern what is specifically moral, and thus what is the ideal aim. Nonetheless, it is conceivable and possible to become sensitive to specific types of subjective forms such as moral obligation. Therefore, it is possible to develop a sensitivity to one's ideal aim.

Hence, an alternative approach to moral decisions determined through rational calculation is a moral life guided by conscience, that is, a life guided by direct responsiveness to the ideal aim. By not holding any one approach to ethics as definitive, Cobb seems to recognize both that there is a continuity between these emphases in the moral life, and that most persons incorporate all of these emphases into their moral reasoning. Moreover, in spite of the difficulties of discernment that necessarily accompany a morality of conscience—difficulties which mitigate against the possibility of a purely passive openness to the ideal aim—this theory of conscience provides cosmological support for a Christian ethics which attempts to understand the moral life as direct response to God's activity.

In summary, I have noted thus far that Cobb's theory of obligation leads to an ethic of rational determination. However, this rationalistic ethic leaves open the question of what is relevant to one's moral decision. Hence, Cobb gives a cosmological account of value as beauty as one highly relevant factor in making moral decisions. Because obligation and value originate from the same root, namely, the ideal aim provided to each occasion by God, Cobb's account of value makes an important step toward a type of concrete ethic neglected by his theory of obligation, for in addition to the rationalistic approach to the moral life, Cobb notes the possibility of a life guided directly by the ideal aim experienced as conscience.

However, Cobb presses further in developing a concrete ethic by examining what is unique to human responsibility and Christian ethics. Specifically, Cobb examines the nature of personal responsibility and the virtue of love. Hence, I turn to Cobb's character theory.

CHARACTER THEORY

Inasmuch as character theory focuses more upon the nature or "being" of the agent (cf. Frankena 1973, 63 f.), rather than upon the principles or rules of action, Cobb's theory of obligation, and hence the basis of his early ethical theory, could be reinterpreted as a theory of character. This reinterpretation seems possible to the extent that process cosmology understands the being of an actual occasion as equivalent to its activity or its becoming (cf. Whitehead 1978, 23). Put differently, an actual occasion *is* its decision or self-creation out of its prehensions of past occasions (Whitehead 1978, 43). Thus, the character of the actual occasion can be said to determine the nature of its actions. However, such an interpretation does not really do justice to the early formation of Cobb's theory of obligation which, as I have shown, emerges out his concern to demonstrate that the ground of ethics is independent of theological and cosmological considerations. Moreover, such an approach to character theory does not really elucidate what is unique to human persons as moral agents. Hence, it is also important to understand Cobb's character theory as it applies to personal responsibility over time.

Basic to Cobb's understanding of personal responsibility is his view of freedom as "self-determination." Cobb, with Whitehead, believes that all actual occasions have some degree of freedom: "freedom is a universal or categorical feature of all actual entities whatsoever" (1965a, 94). Human freedom is thus a "special case" of the freedom found in all actual occasions (1965a, 94). The freedom of an actual occasion is not without limits, for as we have seen, every occasion must take into account the "settled conditions" of its past, and receives novelty from God as the principle of limitation. Thus, the occasion's freedom is bounded by the causally efficacious world preceding it and by the possibilities provided by God through the scaled set of eternal objects that make up the initial aim. However, it is because God provides a scaled set of relevant possibilities for realization that freedom is possible. An occasion modifies and adapts the initial aim provided by God to form its subjective aim by choosing from this set of relevant possibilities those which it will actualize (1965a, 95 f.). Put differently, an occasion's freedom "lies in its own self-determination as to just *how* it will take account of all [past] occasions" (1965a, 95). Thus, the individual occasion's modification of its own subjective aim is the final locus of freedom (1965a, 96).

Cobb's view of freedom, like his theories of obligation and value, focuses primarily upon individual, momentary, actual occasions, rather than upon persons who live and act over innumerable moments. This tendency is due in part to Cobb's cosmological conviction that the locus of freedom, decision, and value is the individual occasion of experience. However, this tendency raises some questions for understanding human moral experience because human moral experience spans many occasions of experience, whether it be the 30 seconds it takes to perform an act deemed morally right or whether it be the lifetime it takes to cultivate certain dispositions deemed morally good.

In particular, the question is raised as to the nature of personal identity and responsibility relative to individual occasions over time. If the identity of each individual occasion is wholly discrete, it would be meaningless to assign moral responsibility to a present individual for an act or decision of one of its predecessors. In fact, since Whitehead assumes that only individual occasions have total self-identity (1965a, 71), it would seem that at most he could conclude that an individual actual occasion can only be responsible for it own concrescence. Cobb's account of the possibility of personal identity, and thus personal responsibility, among the manifold occasions which make up the human moral agent is prerequisite to his theory of character inasmuch as any theory character focuses upon the cultivation of dispositions, that is, the acquisition over time of traits or styles of behavior (Frankena 1973, 63).

For Cobb, the human moral agent is a living person, and a living person is a soul (1965a, 50). The soul refers to the serially ordered dominant occasions of a structured society of occasions through time. The dominant occasion of a structured society such as a highly developed animal or a human being has several characteristics: (a) it is a living occasion—an occasion characterized more by its prehension of eternal objects than by its prehension of past occasions, that is, by the presence of novelty in the occasion (Cobb

1965a, 42; Whitehead 1978, 102); (b) it has a high degree of mentality, making it the only type of occasion that is conscious (1965a,
49); (c) it provides centralized control or dominance over the society
(1965a, 49); and (d) it is located in the environment of the brain
which mediates feelings from the body to the dominant occasion
(1965a, 52). Of course, not all structured societies of occasions have
dominant occasions. For example, most plants are "democracies" of
occasions, in which the life of the society is directed generally toward
the enrichment of all its occasions (1965a. 43). But in most higher
animals, especially human beings, the dominant occasion is that occasion which is the center of the experiences arising from that
society.

The serially ordered dominant occasions which make up the
soul are also a society. But, unlike the structured society of which it
is the center, none of the soul's members is contemporary. In other
words, the structured society of occasions which make up a particular
human being through time is presided over by an enduring object or
serially ordered society of dominant occasions. The question of personal identity, and hence of responsibility, revolves around how the
later occasions of a serial order can be said to have identity with
earlier occasions in that order. This is generally not a question for all
other types of enduring objects in which the constitutive occasions
maintain identity through repetition of common characteristics. Put
differently, most enduring objects are made up of occasions which
prehend their predecessors in terms of their physical poles, and thus
in terms of causal efficacy. This form of identity displays great conformity, but trivializes freedom, novelty, and mentality, and thus
displays little life (1965a, 50).

What gives the enduring object of the soul its identity or
personal order is the way each successive dominant occasion in the
serial order embodies or prehends the previous occasions making up
that society so as to maintain continuity without sacrificing novelty,
mentality, and life (1965a, 50). Specifically, the soul is made up of
occasions which are constituted by hybrid prehensions of their predecessors. Thus, the occasions of the soul prehend their predecessors in
terms of their conceptual poles as well as their physical poles, that
is, in terms of the novelty embodied in the previous occasions
(1965a, 51). Where the occasions of other types of enduring objects
maintain continuity through repetition of their physical prehensions,
(thus "trivializing . . . novelty or mentality"), the occasions of the

soul maintain continuity by summing up the past of the society "with some peculiar completeness," adding to their prehensions of past novelty their own novelty, "compounding the richness of the inheritance of successive occasions" (1965a, 51).

Cobb revises Whitehead's understanding of personal identity by speculating upon the nature of hybrid prehensions (1965a, 76-78). Pure physical prehensions which are in the mode of causal efficacy, say the prehension of occasions in the nerve endings in the eye by occasions of brain, are mediated through contiguous events. Whereas hybrid prehensions of the dominant occasions, which occur via the conceptual pole as well as the physical pole, allow immediate prehension of all past occasions in the soul. Thus, in a physical prehension only the contiguous events are prehended directly and the mediated events are prehended indirectly. Whereas, in a hybrid prehension, it is possible that all past events of the soul are prehended directly through their conceptual poles. This directness is what Cobb interprets as the "peculiar completeness of summing up" by the dominant occasions of their predecessors.

Cobb finds support for this speculation in the common experience of memory. For example, I experience as my own my decision to write a sentence in the previous chapter because I prehend the event of that decision directly in conjunction with a multitude of other past decisions. However, I experience mediately the decision of a colleague to type a sentence, via physical prehensions in the mode of causal efficacy, which begins with the visual perception of my colleague typing and runs along the path of the nervous system to the brain, finally to be prehended by my dominant occasion. I do not prehend my colleague's decision directly via the conceptual pole, but indirectly via the physical environment of my body. I prehend my colleague's decision "from without," and mine "from within." I have self-identity with those occasions which I actually or potentially remember from within. Hence, "personal identity obtains whenever there is a serially ordered society of primarily mental occasions (a soul) in which each occasion actually or potentially prehends unmediatedly the mental poles of all its predecessors" (1965a, 79). The definition of personal responsibility follows directly from this account of personal identity: an individual has responsibility for any past acts or decisions of occasions in the individual's serially ordered society which it actually or potentially prehends unmediatedly.

Before looking at the significance of this account of person-hood for character theory, it is important to note briefly the unique-ness of human persons vis à vis other animals. Cobb does not be-lieve that there is a fixed human nature setting human beings apart from animals. Nor does the possession of freedom or the possession of a soul make human beings absolutely unique. For both Cobb and Whitehead, all actual occasions have some degree of freedom, and many, if not most, animals have souls.

However, compared to other souls, the human soul displays much greater freedom and unity of experience, which in turn allows greater richness of experience. The freedom of human occasions of experience is heightened because they possesses self-awareness. In other words, human occasions of experience are actually or po-tentially conscious of their self-determination. Because of this self-awareness, Cobb views human beings as uniquely moral animals (1965a, 97). Moreover, it is clear that many low-grade animals have little unity of experience because these animals function pretty much as vegetables except when there is need for some centralized coor-dination of their behavior (1965a, 57). Even in higher animals, past occasions of the soul are likely to be prehended mediately; that is, they have little experience of memory (1965a, 57 f.).

Nonetheless, some higher animals do seem to have a sig-nificant experience of memory, and possibly of self-awareness and freedom—certainly, more than that of a human infant. For this reason, Cobb finds that the important distinction between human beings and other animals rests with humans' *potentiality* for novelty, and hence for complexity and richness of experience. For example, an adult orangutan probably has greater richness of experience than a human infant, but, barring cases of deformity, the human infant has potential for even greater richness of experience. This potential, made possible by a higher development of consciousness, is demon-strated, as well as furthered, by language, morality, and historicality, that is, "the potential for being formed by history" (1965a, 62 f.). Notwithstanding this potential, it is clear that Cobb assumes a quantitative difference between the type of identity and richness of experience found among human and animal occasions of experience.

Cobb's account of personal identity provides a way to inter-pret his theory of conscience as indicating an ideal character type. In terms of the individual dominant occasions of the human soul, each dominant occasion prehends (a) the causally efficacious past (e.g., of the body); (b) the past occasions making up the soul; and (c) the ideal aim provided by God. Cobb argues that the occasions of the past—those of the world and those of the soul—also embody specific aims for the present dominant occasion (1965a, 182 f., 248). God's ideal aim and the aims of the past form a composite aim—an initial aim—for the present dominant occasion. According to Cobb's theory of conscience, when the individual dominant occasion is able to discern the ideal aim from among the conflicting aims, that is, when it is able to discern what is ideally right in the given moment, it is able to actualize the ideal aim. Because of the personal identity between the present occasion of the soul and its predecessors, the aims of the predecessors are prehended with particular force. Consequently, if these aims are in tension with the ideal aim, the present dominant occasion will have difficulty in conforming itself to the ideal aim. Conversely, if these aims are supportive of the ideal aim—that is, if they aim at conformity to the ideal aim—then the present occasion will have a disposition to the ideal aim. Put differently, the individual occasions of the soul increasingly aim to conform the subjective aim of their future self to the ideal aim. An ideal character type is implied by the possibility of progressively cultivating among the occasions of the soul an aim to be predisposed to conform to the ideal aim. The "cumulative result" of these progressive decisions is the achievement of "a kind of natural and unforced dominance" of God's aim for the occasion (1965a, 249 f.). Cobb calls this character type the "saint" (1965a, 250).

Cobb does not go into much detail about the nature of the saint, but one can speculate, on the basis of Cobb's moral theory, what some of the ingredients of sainthood are. Inasmuch as the ideal aim for any occasion aims at greater richness of experience; and inasmuch as an increase in consciousness, particularly self-awareness, brings about greater potential for freedom and personal identity which, in turn, brings an increase in richness of experience; each dominant occasion of the soul ought to aim at greater consciousness for itself and its successors, and hence at greater potential for freedom and a sense of identity.

As consciousness of the ideal aim is cultivated, it would seem that one would experience a tension. On the one hand, one would have an increasing awareness of the ideal aim as immanent in each moment of experience, yet transcending that experience. Cultivation of this awareness presumably would lead to an awareness of the source of the ideal aim, namely, God, along with an increasing awareness of one's dependence upon God. On the other hand, one would have a growing sense of personal identity and freedom which would lead to a heightened awareness of one's personal responsibility and self-determination. The tension between one's independence and responsibility as a self-determining agent and one's dependence upon God as the source of one's being is intensified as awareness of the ideal aim—and thus self-awareness—is cultivated.

In *The Structure of Christian Existence*, Cobb points to a similar tension. The early Christians' experience of God as immanent Spirit brought about an existential awareness both of responsibility for one's inner motives as the source of one's actions and of one's inability to determine all one's inner motives—and thus, one's dependence upon God for aid (1967b, 120 f.).

> Somehow, the Christian knew himself as responsible for choosing to be the kind of self he was, even when he found that his desire to change himself into another kind of self was ineffectual. Hence, he [realized that] the divine Spirit ... could do within him something which he could not do in and for himself. ... The Christian had to accept a responsibility for his existence as a whole in a way that separated him from Judaism. This meant that he must understand himself as transcending his will in the sense of his power of choice among practicable alternatives in a given situation. He was responsible not only for his choice but also for the motive of his choosing. He was responsible for being the kind of self who could not will to choose to have the motive he should. (1967b, 121)

In this description of the emergence of the structure of Christian existence, the self transcends its own self-determination and recognizes its radical responsibility for itself, achieving what Cobb refers to as a "self-transcending selfhood" or spiritual existence. At the same time, without repudiating its responsibility, the self recognizes that it ultimately has no control over that for which it is responsible, and it recognizes its dependence upon the divine initiative if it is to be able to do that which it cannot do by its own will.

Assuming, thus far, that these speculations on the nature of sainthood are consistent with Cobb's account of personal identity and the initial aim, it seems that description of the tension between one's sense of responsibility and self-determination and one's sense of dependence upon God is essentially the same as Cobb's description of the rise of spiritual existence which emerged with Christianity.[6] If so, then these speculations on sainthood can be pursued by turning to Cobb's understanding of the emergence of Christian existence.

First, it must be noted that Cobb makes a distinction between spiritual existence and Christian existence. The achievement of spiritual existence only brings about the recognition of the tension between self-determination and dependence upon God, thus making possible a higher synthesis or fulfillment. However, the tension between self-determination and dependence upon God also makes possible a vicious circle of self-preoccupation (1967b, 134). According to Cobb, the only escape from self-preoccupation—thus, fulfillment of the tension between self-determination and dependence upon God—comes through Christian existence, which is to say, through spiritual existence expressed in love (1967b, 134 f.).

In its most basic form, love is present wherever there exists spontaneous concern of one entity for other entities (1967b, 125), which we have noted is the concern to contribute to future occasions, both those belonging to one's projected personal order and others. Cobb believes that all entities are capable of some form of love, but for human persons at the level of axial existence, Cobb understands love as an "autonomous activity of the psyche" (1967b, 126).

There are various forms of love which correspond to the various structures of axial existence. Cobb states that in all forms of axial existence love refers to "any mode of relatedness to an object as a positive intrinsic value, in which conscious psychic activity is decisively involved" (1967b, 127). By "intrinsic value," Cobb seems to depart from his definition in *A Christian Natural Theology* as the satisfaction an entity achieves in itself. Rather, "intrinsic value" seems to include the value the object has for the subject, independently of other values the object brings about for the subject (see 1967b, 127 ff.). Hence, Cobb notes that in Greek existence and prophetic existence love did not overcome human beings' natural self-centeredness of feeling. For example, among the four types of love that Cobb ascribes to the Greeks—desire, adoration, aesthetic admiration, and friendship—desire "was the attending to the object [loved] as that which provided satisfactions to the subject"; adoration produced in the subject pleasure of "being possessed rather than from possessing"; aesthetic admiration was the subject's enjoyment of the object's "perfection of form" independently of any desire to possess the object or to be possessed by it; and even friendship, which involved desire for the object's good, was seen as a means to and limited by the subject's own desire for happiness (1967b, 127-29).

Love in prophetic existence made a large step toward transcending self-centeredness. Here love emerged primarily as obedience to the will of a personal God. The "I-Thou" relationship which ensued forced a profound recognition of the distinction "between love of the other and love of self" because the other was recognized as having his or her own ends (1967b, 131). Because God was experienced as the supreme other, the Hebrews recognized that love of God took precedence over self-love. In addition, because "the deeper reality of all things was to be found in God's perception of the world," the Hebrews recognized that one's neighbor and oneself were essentially the same. Consequently, "one should love one's neighbor as oneself" (1967b, 132). This meant to seek the good of the other for the other's sake. Nevertheless, this demand was experienced as a demand upon one's will, and thus seeking the good of the other for the other's sake was generally subsumed under one's own motive of seeking righteousness (1967b, 132). Hence, human natural self-centeredness remained as love of God and neighbor was understood as a means to one's own righteousness.

With the advent of Christian existence, love of God and neighbor remained central, but they were transformed by the new awareness of one's responsibility, not only for one's action, but also for one's motives—even for one's natural self-centeredness of feeling. Love as seeking the good of the other for the other's sake was no longer mere obedience of the will or a means to righteousness, for no willing or action could be sufficient if it did not express the right attitude. Rather, love was understood as an attitude or "state of feeling" that gives rise to willing and action (1967b, 133). As a state of feeling, love of others comes into conflict with the natural self-centeredness of feeling. Thus, the demand of love goes beyond the demand of righteousness so as to fulfill the demand of righteousness.

However, if love is no longer under the control of the will, then one cannot simply decide to love the other without regard to the effect of that love on oneself. To make such a deliberate effort would not only destroy the spontaneity which characterizes all forms of love, it would also intensify preoccupation with oneself, exacerbating one's natural self-centeredness of feeling. In Cobb's words, "Every effort to love, in order to break out of the misery of self-preoccupation, is also an expression of the self-preoccupation and is condemned to intensify it" (1967b, 135). This is the vicious circle made possible by spiritual existence. Love in Christian existence, therefore, cannot be a product of the will. Rather, only if love somehow precedes and determines the will can there be fulfillment of spiritual existence. Hence, the love that characterizes Christian existence cannot be achieved by oneself—it is "unattainable by [one's] own efforts" (1967b, 135).

Cobb concludes that only if one is "freed from the necessity to love," will one find salvation from self-pre-occupation (1967b, 135). This means that only as one knows oneself as already loved in one's self-preoccupation—already accepted in one's sin and sickness—can one escape one's self pre-occupation. For as one knows oneself as loved in one's sinfulness, one no longer is under the necessity to love in order to save oneself from self-preoccupation, and thus one is free to love others as they are for their own sakes (1967b, 135). In other words, the experience of God's love for us in our most profound sin of self-preoccupation frees us from our self-preoccupation so that we can love with genuine concern for the other without regard for ourselves.

Love of others without regard to any merit for oneself implies an ideal of personal, yet impartial love. Personal, because the individual, not what the individual produces for the subject, is the object of the love. Impartial, because if love is independent of the merits of the one loved, no one merits love more than any other. Such an ideal, as Cobb notes, is "superhuman" (1965a, 247). Not surprisingly, Cobb notes that "no Christian should lay claim to any simple embodiment of such love" because nearly every person is made up of a complexity of feeling that includes instinct, unconscious motives, and self-seeking (1967b, 135). However, "the whole can be, and often is, redeemed by the presence of an element of genuine concern for the other as a person" (1967b, 135).

It is interesting to note that when Cobb talks about impartiality, he confines himself primarily to human beings in his pre-1969 ethics. But already, on the level of theory, it would appear that impartial love is an ideal that can be extended to all individuals, including non-humans. In fact, even in his early writings, Cobb identifies impartial love with love of "life as life" (1965a, 127). This theoretical possibility suggests a continuity between Cobb's pre-1969 ethics, which does not address ecological issues, and his post-1969 ethics, in which the ecological crisis becomes the central issue. Nonetheless, before 1969, Cobb's understanding of the virtue of impartial love which characterizes sainthood remains restricted to humanity.

Cobb suggests that the ideal of sainthood is approached and reinforced by love of God, because "if God is truly loved, then all that comes from [God] and returns to [God] must be loved also for its own sake" (1965a, 247). This conclusion follows from Cobb's description of God whose own achievement of beauty is identical to God's seeking and contributing to maximal beauty possible for each occasion as God's own achievement of beauty. In other words, God is concerned for each individual impartially and personally. To love God then is to seek for the maximal beauty possible for God in each moment, and therefore to seek for maximal beauty possible for every occasion in each moment.

The key features of the ideal character of the saint can now be summarized. In large part, the character of the saint is identical to life in the Christian structure of existence expressed in love. This life is not the result of passive openness to the ideal aim of God, although it does require a certain receptiveness on the part of the individual (1965a, 130). Rather, the character of the saint grows out of a cultivated awareness of one's identity and self-determination, on the one hand, and of God's immanent activity, on the other. The tension produced by this growing self-awareness reflects a new structure of existence—spiritual existence—which opens up great possibilities of self-centeredness as well as regard for others. Only the realization that one is loved in one's self-centeredness frees one to love others. Cobb believes this has been made possible in the Christian structure of existence.

In the Christian structure of existence, one cannot love because it is one's duty; one can only love because one is first loved by God (1967b, 135). Love, then, can be called a "theological" virtue in the sense that, in the last resort, it cannot be cultivated, but only received as a gift from God. At the same time, receiving this gift does not remove responsibility for one's natural self-centeredness; in fact, one's acceptance of God's love is an admission of responsibility. Thus, the tension between the sense of responsibility and self-determination and the sense of dependence upon God are preserved in a higher synthesis. Love transcends righteousness and duty and finds its proper object in God and in all that comes from God and returns to God (1965a, 247).

CONCLUSIONS

ETHICS AND THEOLOGICAL METHOD

As we have seen, Cobb's earliest attempt at ethical theory originates in his search for an independent, non-speculative ground for theological method. To this end, Cobb first demonstrates that there are universal normative principles which are warranted by empirically verifiable statements. Hence, the aim of Cobb's early ethical theory parallels the aim of his early theological method. Where theological method aims at elucidating beliefs so as to be consistent with empirical knowledge and experience, ethics aims at discovering universal normative principles that are warranted by empirically verifiable statements.

Cobb's earliest formulation of a universal normative ethic—namely, "one ought to consider all available knowledge and experience that appears to one to be relevant"—is too formal to be an adequate ground for theological method. Indeed, Cobb's ethic, like his theological method, requires responsible speculation in order to be relevant to concrete experience. For Cobb, this means that ethics, like theology, requires Whiteheadian cosmology.

Moreover, from a Whiteheadian cosmological perspective, religious experience and moral experience are fundamentally rooted in the same reality, namely, God's ideal aim or "call forward" for the individual. Not surprisingly, the demands of faith and morality converge. A right relationship to God entails the betterment of all creatures, for a right relationship with God is a decision to conform to God's ideal aim, and God aims at contributing to the ideal strength of beauty of all creatures. Put differently, to serve God is to serve others (1965a, 246 f.). Thus, although Cobb does not specifically present his overall ethical theory as a Christian or theological ethic, it can be concluded, in light of his overall method, that his ethical theory is ultimately a theological ethic.

The heart of Cobb's theological ethic is his character theory, namely, growth in the Christian structure of existence. To say that Cobb's character theory is the heart of his theological ethic is not to ignore the balance of Cobb's overall ethic. I have shown that the nature of obligation, value, and character are intimately interwoven. However, Cobb, himself, states that the ethics of love fulfills duty (1965a, 127), and he notes that the ethics of the saint—natural conformity to God's ideal aim—is humanity's true end (1965a, 250 f.). Moreover, as I noted in the previous chapter, Cobb conceives the furthering of the Christian structure of existence as the mission of the church, and for this reason I take this ideal character to be the heart of Cobb's Christian ethics.

SOCIAL ETHICS

The centrality of character theory to Cobb's theological ethic raises some questions for social ethics. Insofar as Cobb's ethic centers on character, the central moral issue appears to be primarily the perfection of one's inner self and motivation. One's relationship to society appears secondary to self perfection, and the question of social and political change is not even raised.

As noted in the previous chapter, Gustafson is critical of character theory—especially an ethic of sanctification—because it turns persons inward to themselves: "The Christian becomes preoccupied, not with the objective work of Christ, but with his [or her] own state" (1968, 81). Given Cobb's description of the Christian structure of existence as giving "radical priority to the inner state," the importance of social responsibility may seem less significant than personal perfection (1967b, 114).

However, Cobb seems to recognize Gustafson's criticism when he notes that only the experience of God's love can rescue one from the vicious circle of self-preoccupation. Cobb's ideal of personal perfection is not one of individual achievement. Rather, it is an ideal of love for others. Moreover, for Cobb, the self is not an independently self-subsisting substance that can be molded in isolation from the wider community. The self is cosmologically and historically a socially constructed self that is always formed in relation to all actuality, in particular to God, and it inescapably contributes to all other actualities, especially to God. Put differently, any actual occasion is affected by all actual occasions that have occurred before it, and whatever any actual occasion does affects all subsequent actual occasions. One cannot completely ignore that one's choices will either contribute positively or negatively to the welfare of the larger society. In fact, to become more aware of the social effects of one's actions contributes to one's ability to maximize value for oneself and others, because self-consciousness increases freedom, which, as we noted above, increases the potential for value. Hence, Cobb's Whiteheadian understanding of the social character of actual entities points to a fundamental acceptance of the contention that it is impossible to have a "private ethic" which does not also have profound social consequences.

Still it is important to ask, as McCann asks of Reinhold Niebuhr's theological ethics, whether a "dispositional ethic," even when applied to politicians and social activists, is a sufficient basis for social ethics (McCann 1982). Cobb's attempt to work out a social ethics will be examined and evaluated more fully in the next three chapters. However, it is worth noting here, that on the formal level, that is, on the level of Cobb's theory of obligation, the central obligation to consider relevant knowledge and experience, in principle, implies consideration of the nature of the social and political processes which affect and are affected by human decisions. The implied relevance of social and political processes to moral choices, coupled with an organismic understanding of the interrelatedness of entities in even trivial decisions, points to the necessity of social responsibility. Hence, although at this stage of Cobb's thought the nature and extent of a Christian social ethics is yet to be formulated, some theoretical basis for social ethics has been laid.

CHRISTOLOGY AND ETHICS

Throughout his discussion of ethics, there is a noticeable absence of the role of christology in the formulation of Cobb's ethical theory—even his theological ethics. As I noted in the previous chapter, even in Cobb's discussion of the structure of Christian existence, the role of Christ in the formation of this new existence can be viewed pretty much as an historical contingency. That is, the historical person Jesus Christ was responsible for the initial emergence of the Christian structure of existence, but that existence can occur today among those who know little or nothing of Jesus Christ. Cobb does say that the "Christian's ideal of love is formed by Jesus Christ" and implies that Jesus' love is a measure of the Christian's (1967b, 138). But, theologically, the more important measure of love seems to be the Consequent Nature of God which is prehended as

God's love for the world flowing back into the world (1965a, 230). Christ plays hardly any continuing role in the development of Christian existence, and hence has only peripheral significance for Christian ethics.

NOTES

1. For example, Cobb was active in the Democratic Club during the 1960's as well as actively opposed to U.S. involvement in Vietnam (John B. Cobb, Jr., interview, 19 July, 1984).

2. Although only published in 1986, this paper was written and presented in 1970 for a conference on ethics held at Catholic University of America (John B. Cobb, Jr., letter, 6 August , 1986). This paper parallels the section "An Ethical Theory" in *A Christian Natural Theology* and does not discuss the ecological issues in which Cobb had only just taken interest. For that reason, I take the paper as representative of Cobb's pre-1969 development.

3. Cobb actually puts all these factual warrants in Whiteheadian terminology. e.g., "When one endeavors to reach a decision, the sense of obligation is inescapably included in the subjective form of the imaginative feeling of oneself giving full consideration to whatever knowledge and experience appear relevant" (1965a, 119) Cobb uses the Whiteheadian terminology to clarify how the sense of obligation attaches to one's entertainment of a possibility for action of which one is the actor. I bracket its usage here for systematic reasons, viz., to indicate the reasons why Cobb eventually turns to Whitehead in his developed ethics.

4. As far as I know, Cobb does not use the terms "character theory" or "virtue theory" in discussing his anthropology. But it is clear that he espouses a normative view of human nature that is fundamental to ethical development, which, for the sake of clarity, I call character or virtue theory.

5. Cobb tends to make a distinction between ethics as rational calculation based upon the universal normative principle and direct responsiveness to the ideal aim (see 1965a, 127 ff., 247; 1986b, 29). In addition, Cobb contrasts love, as spontaneous and personal, with ethics, as calculating and disinterested. (I examine the role of love in Cobb's ethics below.) Inasmuch as I am interested in analyzing Cobb's *theological* or Christian ethics, I have chosen to subsume the "rational ethical," the normative aspects of direct responsiveness to the ideal aim, and love under the more inclusive rubric of Cobb's Christian ethics. In doing so, I do not intend to refute or minimize

Cobb's distinctions; rather, I want lift up the coherence of Cobb's theological ethics.

6. Cobb does not explicitly make this identification anywhere that I know. As stated in the preceding note, Cobb implies that there is a distinction between conscience or responsiveness to the ideal aim and love—which is the virtue implied by the Christian structure of existence (see 1965a, 127 ff., 247). My speculation is an attempt to show that there is, nevertheless, an underlying continuity between saintliness and the Christian structure of existence fulfilled in love.

CHAPTER THREE

ECOLOGY AND THE TRANSFORMATION OF THEOLOGICAL ETHICS

In the first two chapters I surveyed and analyzed the background and development of Cobb's theology and ethics before 1969. Cobb takes as his starting point for theological method the essence of the Christian vision or the abstract ideal of the primitive witness of Christian faith found in the New Testament as that is determined historically. Although the role and meaning of Jesus Christ is important to theological method insofar as Jesus Christ was the historical occasion of faith, and insofar as beliefs about Jesus Christ pose possible obstacles to faith, Cobb's historical analysis of the Christian witness leads him to identify the abstract ideal or essence of Christianity with the structure of Christian existence rather than with some aspect of Jesus Christ. Nonetheless, Cobb's theological method can be called a *"Christian natural theology"* insofar as it employs Whiteheadian cosmology to relate a Christian vision of the world to contemporary, empirical knowledge and experience so as to nurture faith and overcome doubt.

The starting point of Cobb's ethical reflection is an analysis of the basic experience of obligation which determines that we ought to do that which appears right upon consideration of relevant knowledge and experience. In order to clarify what knowledge and experience are universally relevant, Cobb finds it necessary to turn again to Christian natural theology. Hence, the central normative category that emerges in Cobb's Christian ethics to this point coin-

71

cides with the essence of the Christian vision, namely, the Christian structure of existence. Not surprisingly, then, Jesus Christ has almost an incidental role in Cobb's ethics. Moreover, even though Cobb's early ethical theory is open to development in relation to social issues, his early ethical writings seldom deal with substantive issues in social ethics.

Cobb's awakening to the ecological crisis in 1969 profoundly affected his theological and ethical thinking. In his contribution to *The Christian Century*'s 1980 "How My Mind Has Changed" series, Cobb goes so far as to say that in the summer of 1969, he underwent a "conversion experience" when he realized that not only was the ecological crisis rapidly leading to "global self-destruction," but that it was rooted in the present structures of technological and socio-economic development that he once thought would ameliorate war, hunger, and injustice (1981a, 74 f.). Cobb became convinced that Christians will not be able to provide a serious, efficacious response to the ecological crisis unless they "move forward to a new form of Christianity" (1972b, Preface).

In this chapter, I examine how Cobb's subsequent theological and ethical reflection attempts to move to a new form of Christianity by revising his Christian ethics and theological method. I argue that the ecological crisis is not merely an issue responded to within the given framework of Cobb's earlier Christian ethics; rather, it has led to a transformation of Cobb's christology, which, in turn, has transformed his theological ethics and his method.

THE ECOLOGICAL CRISIS AND THE FAILURE OF THE CHRISTIAN STRUCTURE OF EXISTENCE

For over a century, the ethos of technological and socio-economic development has encouraged and supported the progressive industrialization and urbanization of the northern and, more recently, of the southern hemispheres, which is blindly exterminating entire species of animals, polluting water and air, and destroying vast areas of both rain forests and arable land—all for the short-term gain of economic wealth and increased consumption. Cobb's recognition that the ecological crisis is rooted in the structures of our technological and socio-economic ethos poses a radical challenge for all

Christian ethics insofar as Christianity has helped to spawn and continues to undergird this ethos.

In his first major work on ecology, *Is It Too Late? A Theology of Ecology* (1972b), Cobb notes that Christianity's traditional interpretation of the world as creation and subject to human domination provided a world view that has encouraged the development of science and technology. To see the world as the creation of a purposeful and intelligent Being allowed thinkers to see the world as ordered rationally, and thus "provided the context and motivation for the sustained and patient effort, divorced from all consideration of practical results, that carried Western European science from its infancy in the Middle Ages to the amazing achievements of the seventeenth century" (1972b, 34).

Moreover, the conviction that humanity is created in God's image and given "dominion" over the rest of creation has led to the belief that only human beings have intrinsic worth, while the subhuman world has merely instrumental value (1972b, 35). By its view that the subhuman world is a mere means to be manipulated for human consumption and pleasure, this belief has encouraged the development of the technological attitude. In addition, the absolutization of the value of human life which follows from this belief has contributed to the population explosion inasmuch as this absolutization has encouraged efforts to conquer disease and prolong human life without thought for the capacity of the environment to sustain that life (1972b, 35).

To the extent that this portrayal of Christianity is accurate, the ecological crisis fundamentally calls into question the adequacy and efficacy of Christianity to provide the sort of moral guidance and insight that can ameliorate the conditions which are leading to the destruction of the planet. Nor has modern Western ethics—which also tends to assume a radical gap between human value and the value of the rest of nature—been able to improve upon Christianity in responding to the ecological crisis. Modern ethics is essentially humanistic, and thus, "in both its utilitarian and its Kantian forms, take[s] *man's* good as its unquestioned context" (1972b, 54). Questions of duties, rights, and justice, are pertinent only to human endeavors. The environment puts no claim on human persons except insofar as that claim is derived from the rights of or utility for human beings.

In light of Cobb's recognition of Christianity's contribution to the ethos underlying the ecological crisis, it is not surprising that he also concludes that the development of the Christian structure of existence does not provide an adequate basis for a Christian response to the ecological crisis. The radical self-transcendence of Christian existence so intensifies freedom, individuality, and responsibility, that one is "turned toward God and [one's] fellow man, and [the] natural environment almost loses significance" (1972b, 50). Although Christian existence leads to a high valuation of human life, providing progress toward "an extreme humanism," it also "tends to widen the gulf between man and other living things" (1972b, 51).[1]

The role of Christian existence in widening the gulf between human persons and the environment not only makes self-transcending selfhood an inadequate basis for responding to the ecological crisis, it also makes Christian existence a contributing factor to the ecological crisis as well as to self-interested individualism and ideological blindness.

> Our present structure encourages the externalizing and objectifying of other living things and even of other human beings. It accentuates the competitive element in existence. It juxtaposes private interest to the public good in such a way as to require special exhortation to encourage attention to the latter. This juxtaposition also leads to distortion of the capacity for objective thinking so that even much of what passes for science is tainted by ideology. (1980, 454)

Given this assessment of the impact of Christian existence on how humanity relates to the larger environment, it is not surprising that Cobb believes that,

> A different fundamental attitude is urgently needed. ... This change of attitude can occur only as man gains a sense of kinship with the subhuman world. ... We need to gain an experience of actual participation and interpenetration with our environment. This requires a change in the structure of Christian existence itself. (1972a, 8 f.)

If, however, the Christian structure of existence must be changed, Cobb appears to be faced with a problem. The Christian structure of existence represents both the central normative category of Cobb's Christian ethics and the essence of the Christian vision, which is central to his theological method of Christian natural theology. By what criterion, then, do we change the Christian structure of existence? On the one hand, Christian existence could be altered to respond to the perceived needs of the moment. But to do so raises anew the issue of relativism and whether the superseding existence(s) is (are) indeed an improvement over the traditional form of Christian existence. Moreover, such a criterion of change calls into question how the new existence could be understood as Christian. On the other hand, a norm other than the primitive Christian witness might be found by which the authenticity of a new Christian existence can be determined. However, such a norm—which would have to be more fundamental than the primitive witness of Christian faith—has the potential for being the sort of particularistic, dogmatic proposition or belief that Cobb rejected as an obstacle to faith in the first formulations of his Christian natural theology. Hence, Cobb re-examines the object of the primitive witness of Christian faith, namely, Jesus Christ, in order to find a norm for Christian faith that is able to provide adequate guidance to life and is immune to both exclusivistic dogmatism and vulgar relativism.

CHRISTOLOGY AND ETHICS

Cobb's revision of christology is not only an attempt to provide an understanding of Christ that can direct Christian response to "our endangered planet" by providing "a Way through the chaos of our time" (1975, 24); it is also a self-conscious response to the problem of affirming the salvific and hopeful reality of Christ in the face of secularism and pluralism (1975, 18). Cobb's pre-1969 christology was formulated primarily in terms of the historical nature of Jesus as the unique origin of Christian existence, rather than in terms of the universal or cosmological meaning of Jesus Christ. Consequently, not only was the normative category of the Christian structure of existence incapable of speaking to the present global crisis, Cobb's historical view of Jesus raised the question of how, if

Christianity is only one Way among others, Jesus Christ can have
the ultimacy and universality that Christians claim.

In his pre-1969 christology, Cobb avoided elucidating the
cosmological significance of Christ, for example, as the Word or the
Logos, in distinction from the historical person of Jesus, because he
believed that Christians too often "confused the Jesus in whom God
was distinctly present with God himself" (1975, 13). Cobb's decision is consistent with his empirical attitude and his concern to
avoid the fallacy of misplaced concreteness, that is, the fallacy of
treating abstractions as concrete realities. Often, when one speaks of
Christ as "Word" or "Logos" one is over-concretizing something that
was originally meant as a metaphor, so that the image of Christ may
appear more real than the historical person it is meant to describe.
Hence, the distinctive reality and importance of the historical Jesus is
easily negated by a sort of neo-docetism.

Because his earlier christology started with the historical
figure of Jesus and then asked how this figure embodied the divine,
rather than starting with the eternal divine reality and asking how God
was present in Jesus, Cobb refers to his pre-1969 christology as a
"Jesusology" or a "christology from below" (Cobb & Gier 1970, 22
f.). Although Cobb does not reject his early formulations of the nature of Jesus and his relationship to God, he finds that his early
Jesusology is incomplete, lacking the power of idealist christologies,
such as Thomas Altizer's, to move and inspire Christians so as to
respond to the problems of secularism, pluralism, and global destruction (1975, 14). Thus, Cobb attempts to appropriate elements
of a christology from above—specifically, the notion of Christ as an
image—which he believes to be consistent with his empirical attitude
and capable of inspiring hope and action.

Cobb does not provide a detailed justification for proposing
that Christ can be understood as an image except to say that it is
based, on the one hand, upon Altizer's suggestion that Whitehead's
philosophy is ultimately dependent upon a Christian vision of the
world, specifically upon a christological vision, and on the other,
upon William Beardslee's suggestion that the image of Christ can be
interpreted in Whiteheadian terms as a *proposition* (1975, 14). I believe that this lack weakens Cobb's proposal. However, since Cobb
believes that the notion of Christ as an image resolves the problems
of his earlier Jesusology, it seems worthwhile to supplement Cobb's

view by examining briefly Altizer's and Beardslee's suggestions for understanding the meaning of Christ.

Altizer suggests that process theologians in general, and Cobb in particular, are in peculiar danger of placing christology (and eschatology) at the periphery of faith, and thus are not theological but merely metaphysical, so long as they overlook the implicit christological ground of Whitehead's conception of God (Altizer 1971, 33 f.). Process theologians have failed to recognize that Whitehead's understanding of God as the "ultimate irrationality," "the categorical limitation which does not spring from any metaphysical reason," and about which further knowledge "must be sought in the region of particular experiences," points to a "specifically and uniquely theological ground," namely, "a uniquely Christian empirical and historical ground" (Altizer 1971, 34; cf. Whitehead 1925, 178). Noting that Whitehead, in the last chapter of *Process and Reality*, acknowledges that his view of the consequent nature of God is indebted to the "Galilean vision of God," Altizer asks rhetorically whether Whitehead's view of God is not "indissolubly linked, at least symbolically, with the actual and historical name of Christ?" (Altizer 1971, 35). Altizer concludes that "Whitehead's doctrine of the consequent nature of God is a metaphysical *and* theological conceptualization of the universal, and cosmic, and forward-moving Christ" (Altizer 1971, 37). Thus, Cobb finds in Altizer justification for viewing Whitehead's cosmology not just as a cosmology congenial to the Christian vision of reality, but a cosmology dependent upon and expressing that vision. There may be in Whiteheadian thought itself, then, the elements of a christology.

Cobb believes that Beardslee's thesis that Christ is a proposition provides the Whiteheadian element upon which he can elucidate a christology. A proposition is defined as "a connection of some actual occasion or nexus of actual occasions with some ideal possibility for its realization" (Cobb 1965a, 106). Propositions function primarily as "lures for feeling," that is, as relevant possibilities for realization (Whitehead 1978, 184). Propositions can be understood as *images*, which is to say as "vast and changing clusters of meanings that unite entities and concepts" (Cobb 1975, 65). Cobb asserts that images, especially the great religious images, order our lives and provide direction for our energy (1975, 65). As such, images are neither concrete occasions of experience nor empty abstractions, but rather *hybrid entities* (Whitehead 1978, 185 f.). In fact, Whitehead places propositions, along with actual occasions and eternal objects, among the eight categories of existence (Whitehead 1978, 22). Apparently, then, Cobb believes that viewing Christ as a proposition gives him an ontological justification for exploring the meaning of the image of Christ that avoids the fallacy of misplaced concreteness.

Cobb holds that the name *Christ* is an image which unites the concept of deity with the nexus of actual occasions that constitute the world in general, and Jesus in particular. That is,

> "Christ" does not designate Jesus as such but refers to Jesus in a particular way, namely, as the incarnation of the divine. It does not designate deity as such but refers to deity experienced as graciously incarnate in the world. To abstract the designative element from the conceptual would be to distort the meaning of "Christ" beyond Christian usage. But to abstract the conceptual meaning from the designative one is equally unacceptable. (1975, 66)

It is a mistake to equate Christ with God, on the one hand, because Christ refers to the divine only as it is incarnate in the world; and it is a mistake to equate Christ with the historical Jesus, on the other hand, because Christ refers to Jesus only as he incarnated the divine. Cobb's pre-1969 christology can be described, then, as focusing on the designative element of Christ at the sacrifice of the conceptual element. As we saw in the first chapter, Cobb does discuss the nature of God and the nature of Jesus, and he even suggests a Whiteheadian interpretation of how Jesus was uniquely related to God. However, that discussion of the nature of God is not as a concept united with a nexus of actual entities, but as an actual occasion (or personal order of actual occasions). And Cobb's explanation of God's relationship to Jesus fails to elucidate the ontological significance of what was incarnate in Jesus. The question raised by identifying Christ as a proposition is what aspect of deity do we find incarnate in the world in general, and in Jesus in particular? Cobb turns to the nature of the Logos in Christian tradition to find an answer.

As early as the gospel of John, the aspect of divinity incarnate in Jesus is called the Logos or Word.[2] Through the Logos God makes all things and gives life. In short, the "Logos is the cosmic principle of order, the ground of meaning, and the source of purpose" (1975, 71). Whiteheadian cosmology refers to the creative and ordering aspect of God as God's Primordial Nature; hence, Cobb identifies the Logos with the Primordial Nature of God. For Whitehead and Cobb, God's Primordial Nature is the conceptual pole of God. As such, it is preexisting, eternal, and transcendent. The Primordial Nature of God becomes immanent or incarnate in the world by providing actual occasions with an initial ideal aim at realization. An initial ideal aim is a proposition felt by God, of which the novel occasion is the logical subject, and the appropriate eternal object is the predicate (1965a, 156). Hence, it can be said that through one's prehension of the initial ideal aim, one experiences, to some degree, God's presence in the world.

Because "Christ is the Logos as incarnate" in the world (1975, 71), Cobb identifies Christ as the initial ideal aim (1975, 83). The initial ideal aim is the aim at novel richness of experience or maximal beauty for the occasion and all the occasions to which it contributes. To the extent that the ideal aim is realized by an occasion, it makes a creative advance beyond the past. Christ, then, is the lure toward ideal, novel actualization. As the incarnation of the Logos in the world, Christ makes effectual in actual existence God's envisionment of new possibilities for transforming the past into a new creation, which in turn enriches the future. Put differently, Christ designates the process by which God lures the world toward a richer, more inclusive future by introducing relevant novelties into experience so as to transform discordant elements of past experience into contrasts "in such a way that those elements retain their discrete integrity but attain harmony in a larger whole" (1985a, 7). This process is Christ as *creative transformation*. To identify Christ as creative transformation is to describe the manner in which the Logos was incarnate in Jesus and continues to be incarnate in the world.

When Cobb identifies creative transformation with a cosmological process that occurs at the level of actual occasions, he is not suggesting that we are necessarily unconscious of it in daily experience as we might be unconscious of the movement of electrons in the molecules that make up our body. For example, Cobb notes that creative transformation can readily be discerned in artistic creations, scientific advances, and theological and philosophical insights. It may be helpful to look at a common, though no less dramatic, illustration of creative transformation in human experience alluded to by Cobb, namely, the typical story of alcoholics who join Alcoholics Anonymous (cf. Birch & Cobb 1981, 183).

As noted in the previous chapter, addiction to alcohol or any other drug exemplifies what Whitehead calls "anaesthesia," the aim at repetition of the past which leads to attainment of trivial intensities of experience. Members of Alcoholics Anonymous will often admit that they drank not so much to feel good, but to avoid feeling bad because when they were not drinking they were confronted with pressures and decisions which seemed overwhelming. That is, drinking is an escape from the future, a way of avoiding discord and change. A common testimony of many members of Alcoholics Anonymous is that they came to an awareness that they had "hit bottom," that they were not truly alive, but merely existing. At that point, they admitted that they were alcoholic, and that they were unable to save themselves but were dependent upon a "Higher Power" to lift them out of their situation. Reliance on this Higher Power enables them to accept their past and to become open to a new future, "one day at a time." What is striking to the non-alcoholic is that members of Alcoholics Anonymous do not try to forget their past or turn their back on it; rather they take responsibility for it and continue to refer to themselves as alcoholics even if they have not had a drink in 20 years. The story of these alcoholics' reliance on a Higher Power to turn their lives around describes precisely the process of creative transformation of "discordant elements of past experience into contrasts in such a way as to attain harmony in a larger whole of experience."

It is beyond the scope of this essay to summarize the evidence from art and the history of theology given by Cobb to show how God's presence in the world, in general, and in Jesus, in particular, is experienced as creative transformation. It is interesting to note, however, that Cobb's analysis has precedence in Henry Nelson Wieman's empirical analysis of the source of human good as creative synthesis or the creative good (see Wieman 1946). Unlike Cobb, Wieman, in his determination to avoid any hint of speculation, does not identify the creative good with anything like Whitehead's notion of propositions. Consequently, Wieman is left with the dilemma of either identifying the source of the creative good with the multiplicity of perishing events that display creative transformation, or with what is abstractly common to those events. To take either horn of the dilemma is to call into question the ontological basis of the creative good, and thus whether it can be worthy of devotion. Cobb's understanding of creative transformation as a proposition expressing God's incarnation in the world neither identifies creative transformation with perishing attainments of good, nor with an abstraction, because a proposition, as a hybrid entity, is by definition both concrete and abstract. Hence, Cobb's view of Christ can be read as an attempt at an ontological revision of Wieman's analysis of the creative good that avoids the dilemma posed by Wieman's style of empiricism.

Like Wieman, Cobb believes Christ can be found throughout the secular world as well as in other religious "Ways." In other words, Christ is present to the extent that creative transformation takes place. For example, for Cobb, it does not matter whether members of Alcoholics Anonymous are Christian, Jewish, or Muslim, the Higher Power that makes their transformation possible is for Cobb the power of Christ. Cobb's conviction of the universality of Christ is supported by the Whiteheadian doctrine that the initial ideal aim is realized by each occasion to some extent, even if fragmentarily, because the initial ideal aim, at minimum, determines not only the original directionality of each occasion, but also its locus or standpoint, and therefore which occasions will most directly constitute its past (1965a, 152). Moreover, Cobb suggests that the meaning of Christ is inherently compatible with universality, for "if it is truly Christ who is the center, there can be no boundaries" (1985d, 8). Hence, Cobb believes that every creative advance is made possible by the initial ideal aim, that is, by Christ.

Cobb can be understood, then, to follow the tradition of Logos theologians, such as Clement of Alexandria, which recognizes that the Logos can be incarnate partially in other persons and events, even though the tradition views the Logos as most fully incarnate in Jesus of Nazareth. Hence, Cobb affirms that Christ is universally active in the world, but Jesus *was* the Christ because the Logos, along with Jesus' personal past, co-constituted Jesus' selfhood (1975, 140). This understanding of Christ allows Cobb not only to affirm that Christ is universal and ultimate in spite of both secularism and the competition of many Ways, but also that Christ can be active in secularism and those many Ways. Thus, to be loyal to Christ is to be loyal to Christ's presence even in the secular world or in other Ways, that is, wherever genuine creative transformation takes place.

Although we can discern the work of creative transformation without identifying it with Jesus, recognition of Christ is powerfully augmented by study and familiarity with Jesus and participation in the church that preserves his words and furthers his influence. The New Testament witnesses to how those confronted with Jesus' message and work were creatively transformed. Cobb notes that writers as diverse as the Czech atheist and Marxist, Milan Machovec, and the German theologian, Rudolf Bultmann, attest that Jesus' words creatively transformed Judaism by borrowing from Jewish teaching to radicalize and re-present it so as to give it new meaning (1975, 107). Even today, Christ's message is able to introduce a "permanent principle of restlessness" into our lives which uproots us from complacency, creatively transforming our self-understanding. Cobb notes, as an example, that Luke's parable of the Pharisee and the publican (Luke 18: 10-14), by illustrating how the Pharisee's goodness led to self-congratulation and how the Publican's sinfulness led to humility and openness to God, actually transforms our experience of sinfulness and goodness as mutually exclusive, so that recognition of our sinfulness can be the occasion of justification, and recognition of our goodness can become the occasion of judgment (1975, 108 f.).

More importantly, Cobb emphasizes that Jesus has objective efficacy for creatively transforming the lives of those who believe in him. The apostle Paul attests to this efficacy when he states that as believers we are to put on Christ, live as members of Christ's body, and have new life "in Christ" (Cobb 1975, 116). For Cobb this means that "the real past event of the crucifixion and resurrection of Jesus, involving his total being, has objectively established a sphere of effectiveness or a field of force into which people can enter" (1975, 117). By "field of force" Cobb is simply referring to the way past events are objectified in (or prehended by) present events. Like all past events, the past events of Jesus' life, death, and resurrection are "really, ontologically, effectively ingredient in the constitution of the present" (1975, 121). And like the influence of any past event, Jesus' field of force is enhanced by deliberate attention and memory (1975, 121). However, because Jesus' existence embodied creative transformation, the field of force generated by Jesus' life, death, and resurrection is able to open one to creative transformation to the extent that one "determines how effective that field of force will become in . . . [oneself] and in subsequent entities" (1975, 121). Just as the Logos co-constituted Jesus' self, so conformation to Christ can become "the growing center of one's existence" (1975, 122). By conforming to Jesus Christ, we not only conform to his relationship with God of confidence and openness, thereby becoming children of God and at peace with God, that is, justified in Christ; we also "allow ourselves to be shaped by his righteousness" so that we become increasingly sanctified by God, that is, increasingly creatively transformed (1975, 122 f.).

It is interesting to note that Cobb's analysis of Jesus' field of force is essentially a development of his pre-1969 explanation of how Jesus can be effective in the present. However, in his pre-1969 formulation, Cobb is only concerned with how it is possible that some contemporary Christians seem to experience Jesus, without supposing that such experience is at the heart of faith. Here, however, Cobb presents conformation to the field of force of Jesus Christ as central to the meaning of justification by faith. Indeed, Cobb takes conformation to Christ as the normative ideal of Christian existence. This leads us to the question of how Christ as creative transformation affects Cobb's ethics.

It should be apparent that the identification of Christ with the initial ideal aim recalls Cobb's pre-1969 formulation of the initial ideal aim ethic or ethic of conscience. The ethic of conscience, like life in Christ, consists of conformation to the initial ideal aim. However, Cobb suggests that designating the initial ideal aim as Christ rather than conscience makes a difference as to how one is likely to respond to that aim (1975, 83 ff.). To view the initial ideal aim as conscience connotes "an inner possession or given aspect of the self," thus orienting one toward maintenance of achieved values and self-preoccupation. Attention to the image of Christ, however, makes us aware of the transcendent origin of the initial ideal aim, thus opening us to achievement of new values and other-directedness (1975, 83). Moreover, conscience tends to connote "a static grasp of principles," which implies an ethics of "rigid application of the formal principles of conscience," while "Christ points away from static principles to a dynamic and concrete reality," which implies an ethics of "sensitive openness to Christ" (1975, 84).

More importantly, even where conscience is recognized as creative transformation, originating in the Logos of God, one experiences the Logos as "threatening . . . for it functions to introduce tension between what has been and what might be and continuously to challenge and upset the established order for the sake of the new" (1975, 84). This tension between present and future, between the self and God, recalls Cobb's account of the tension between dependence and independence which gives rise to spiritual existence fulfilled in love. We have seen from the methodological failure of Christian existence that spiritual existence fulfilled in love tends to preserve this tension in a paradoxical existence that exacerbates the opposition between self and others, rather than leading to a genuine synthesis or transformation that creates harmony with others. Cobb suggests that this tension can be overcome when we name the Logos *Christ*. By naming the Logos *Christ*, we recall the incarnation of creative transformation in Jesus who demonstrated "that the divine has constituted itself toward the world once and for all as love" (1975, 85). Thus, in Christ our experience of the Logos as threat becomes a recognition of God as love for all the world.

If Christ is the initial ideal aim, it follows that Christ is the source of moral obligation, and conscious conformity to Christ, rather than the achievement of spiritual existence fulfilled in love, is the Christian's primary moral duty. The "central and normative theological meaning of faith" is no longer self-transcending selfhood, but "the appropriate, primal response to what the divine is and does," namely, "openness to Christ as the new and always coming divine reality" (1975, 88 f.). Elsewhere, Cobb refers to this openness as a new, "deeper meaning of authentic Christian existence" which relativizes self-transcending selfhood (1985a, 6). Not surprisingly, Cobb calls this new existence "Christian existence as Creative Transformation" (1985a, 6). Authentic Christian existence is no longer viewed as self-transcending selfhood because self-transcending selfhood is an historical, not final, achievement of creative transformation, which is itself subject to creative transformation, that is, subject to Christ. Hence, Christ becomes the central normative category in Cobb's revised theological ethics. Life in Christ replaces self-transcending selfhood fulfilled in love as the ideal character type, and Cobb's new ethics becomes a christocentric ethics.

It would be a mistake to read Cobb's turn to Christian existence as creative transformation as a total rejection of the importance of self-transcending selfhood fulfilled in love. Cobb recognizes in self-transcending selfhood a movement toward creative transformation. That is, spiritual existence is a preparatory stage to authentic Christian existence. Although spiritual existence "encourages the externalizing and objectifying of other living things and even of other human beings" (1980, 454), it nevertheless "is one [type of existence] which allows an unusual possibility for becoming aware of what it is, of its contingency, and of the possibility of change" (1980, 452 f.). Thus, spiritual existence has the advantage of being able to criticize itself in light of other forms of existence and thereby to become open to transformation. As spiritual existence becomes open to creative transformation, it becomes an existence in Christ— an existence not merely fulfilled in love, but a life of love.

With the turn to Christian existence as creative transformation, Cobb's view of love is broadened—if not transformed— beyond the ideal of impartial love which fulfills spiritual existence. The ideal of love which fulfills spiritual existence is experienced as a gift from God that allows one to express concern for the other *as other* without regard for oneself, that is, to bring about new, more inclusive values for the sake of others. This ideal is generally understood as applying only to love of other human beings and tends to emphasize what is traditionally called *agape* or "active goodwill" (Cobb & Griffin 1976, 46).[3] *Agape* is "outgoing, assertive, . . . bound up with action," and "oriented to the future rather than toward the past" (1973, 112). Cobb suggests that as long as spiritual existence fulfilled in love is taken as the norm of Christian existence, love is seen as essentially agapic:

> [Spiritual existence] has heightened self-transcendence to the utmost. Christians objectify themselves and assume responsibility both for what they do and for what they are. Thus selfhood is intensified to the highest degree. This makes both possible and necessary the peculiar form of Christian love, *agape*, as concern for the other in her or his otherness. (1975, 208)

Cobb raises the question of whether a strictly agapic view of love can be considered complete or ultimate, especially when it is juxtaposed to the Buddhist ideal of compassion. Indeed, Cobb's interest in broadening the meaning of Christian love, is, in part, a response to the compelling nature of compassion (1975, chap. 13). Unlike *agape* which is predicated on a strong experience of selfhood (albeit self-transcending selfhood), compassion is a letting go of all attachments of the self which overcomes the distinction between the self and the others so that the subject-object dualism of love is replaced by genuine mutuality (1967b, 130). Hence, where *agape* tends to uphold mutual externality of selves, compassion tends to lead to an openness toward all which does not discriminate between others and oneself (1975, 210).

Cobb notes that Christian tradition has long acknowledged that Jesus Christ displayed compassion as well as *agape*. But, in general, compassion was "understood only as the tone of feeling that accompanies *agape*" (1975, 86). Cobb's early theology seems to presuppose this understanding insofar as Jesus is interpreted in light of his role as originating spiritual existence. However, in re-examining the ideal of love embodied in Jesus Christ in the light of his embodiment of creative transformation, Cobb believes that compassion is constitutive of Jesus' love, and not a mere emotional accompaniment. The constitutive character of Jesus' compassion becomes clearer when we recognize that compassion is "empathy," that is, "feeling with others, viewing the situation as they do, allowing one's feelings to conform to theirs" (1975, 86). Although empathy is not active in the conventional sense of the word, it is still efficacious, "for to feel oneself understood by another is already to be helped" (1975, 86). Hence, empathy complements and completes *agape*. While *agape* involves self-constitution "in each moment in relation to the future of the other as well as to [one's] own future," empathy "is a mode of self-constitution that includes the past of the other" (1975, 85, 86).

If we understand Jesus' love to include compassion as well as *agape* and love of God, and if we understand Jesus' love to be an expression of his selfhood, then we can conclude that his love was a form of self-constitution toward the past, toward the future, and toward God. All three aspects of love re-present what has been said about Jesus as the Christ, one whose self was co-constituted by the

Logos. Put differently, Jesus' love reflects the structure of creative transformation philosophically explained in terms of the ideal aim, that is, as incorporation of the past in the movement toward a more inclusive future as that conforms to the divine aim (1975, 86). Christian love, therefore, is an expression of creative transformation.

This view of love as creative transformation implies that the perfection of Christian love would involve conformity to God and others so as to enrich their experience. To conform to God as Logos implies an *imitatio dei*. As love is perfected, one would become increasingly open to the experience of others in one's own self-actualization, yet, at the same time, one would not simply preserve that experience, but would seek, as much as possible through persuasion, to introduce new opportunities for others' self actualization.

> Perfect empathy would open [one's] experience to the entire past and perfect *agape* would open it to the entire future. If all human experience attained this character, diversity [among individuals] would continue, but the separating sense of mine and yours based on the externality of personal selves ... would be transcended in a sense of ours. Whitehead described this condition as "Peace," which "is self-control at its widest—at the width where 'self' has been lost, and interest has been transferred to coordinations wider than personality." (1975, 218)

Clearly, Cobb's revision of christology results in a profound shift in his character theory to a more christocentric view of Christian existence and love. A major reason that Cobb revised his christology was to provide a more adequate basis for a Christian response to the ecological crisis, however, it is interesting to note that although it is implicit in Cobb's analysis of love in *Christ in a Pluralistic Age*, the meaning of love here is not explicitly extended to include the subhuman world—a subdominant theme in Christian history found in Francis of Assisi and Albert Schweitzer (see n. 1 of this chapter). Yet, love as openness to "the entire past" and the "entire future" implies openness to all entities, past and future, and thus to the subhuman (and even non-living) world. Hence, it would seem to follow that Cobb's proposed ideal of love also applies to love of others of the subhuman world, and thus will have significance for an ecological ethic. I will return to this question below in the discussion of Cobb's ecological ethic.

A CHRISTOLOGICAL BASIS FOR AN ECOLOGICAL ETHIC

The central issue for any ecological ethic is what ought to be humanity's relationship to the subhuman world. I have argued that for Cobb the central norm of all Christian ethics is conformation to Christ as creative transformation: the Christian is called to live in responsive openness to creative transformation wherever it occurs. Hence, for Christian ethics, humanity's relationship to the subhuman world is determined by the presence of creative transformation in the subhuman world. Put differently, Cobb believes that Christians are called to conform themselves to the work of Christ in the subhuman world. The questions that arise, then, for a Christian ecological ethic are: How is creative transformation—Christ—present in the subhuman world? and, How are Christians to conform to Christ there?

CHRIST AS LIFE

Cobb answers the first question by showing how creative transformation is at the center of all life. At the cosmological level, creative transformation is present in every actual occasion insofar as God provides it an initial ideal aim at actualization. However, among occasions constituting non-living phenomena, this aim is little more than an aim at repetition of past experiences, and thus the role of creative transformation is trivial compared to the role of causal efficacy. Among occasions constituting living phenomena, the initial ideal aim plays an increasingly decisive role in their concrescence. By introducing a greater degree of novelty into feeling, the initial ideal aim allows these occasions a greater potential for "self-determination" in the sense of having some degree of independence from efficient causal factors (cf. Cobb & Griffin 1976, 67 f.), which, at the same time, allows these occasions to integrate more diverse and contrasting prehensions of the occasions constituting their past world into complex unities of experience, making them capable of greater richness of experience.

These distinctions between non-living and living occasions are not meant to suggest that the boundaries between them can be sharply delineated. "Any line is arbitrary" (Birch & Cobb 1981, 93).

For example, microscopic entities such as certain viruses and mitochondria have properties associated with both living and non-living entities (Birch & Cobb 1981, 91 f.). However, the process of creative transformation plays a more prominent role, and thus is more readily discernable, among the occasions constituting complex living organisms. In short, a creature is more alive to the degree that creative transformation characterizes its experience.

Hence, Cobb identifies creative transformation in the human and subhuman world as the "source of life," which he also refers to simply as *Life*, with an uppercase *L* (Birch & Cobb 1981, 177). Cobb suggests that Wieman's distinction between the creative good and created goods comes very close to capturing the distinction between Life and living things. However, Cobb insists that Life not be understood only as the source of human good, for Life is the source of all richness of experience throughout the living world (Birch & Cobb 1981, 177 ff.).

In *The Liberation of Life*, Cobb uses the name *Life* rather than *Christ*, in part, as a concession to the "publisher [who] wanted more secular language" (1985d, 24). Nevertheless, Cobb notes, this use of the term *Life*, "while not a repetition of Biblical conceptuality, is a faithful witness to the God who in the Bible also is known as Life" (Birch & Cobb 1981, 178). Thus, there is some theological justification for identifying Life with Christ:

> Although the Bible uses many images of the divine, and we too favour doing so, no image is more central than Life. It is closely bound up with both the 'Spirit' and the 'Word.' ... It is the Word which, in the Johanine account, becomes flesh in the Jesus who affirms that he is the Life, the Life which was in the universe from the beginning. (Birch & Cobb 1981, 199 f.)

There is also philosophical justification for identifying Life as Christ. As an image, the meaning of *Christ* is multivalent. Fundamentally, Christ refers to the process of creative transformation which originates with God's lure toward novel actualization. However, the multivalent character of the image of Christ allows Cobb to identify Christ with other aspects of Christian experience,

such as love, which are decisively characterized by creative transformation. The term *Life* not only calls attention to what is of
common value in human and subhuman existence, it is eminently
characterized by creative transformation.

For Cobb, the process of Life as creative transformation is
exhibited in the "strategies of life" or "ecological model of life," that
is, in the evolutionary and ecological processes which have produced
the biosphere, all species of life, including humanity, and their interrelationships. Cobb and Birch take great pains in pointing out that
the process of evolution and ecological relationships are mutually
dependent. Hence, Cobb does not insinuate that Life simply works
through the evolutionary processes as ruthless competition—a crass
version of "survival of the fittest"—for the emergence of "higher"
species is often more the result of successful adaptation to the environment than it is victory over competitors (Birch & Cobb 1981,
65). Nor does he suggest that Life merely aims at some sort of static
"balance of nature," for there are forces for change as well as forces
for stability, as witnessed to by the extinction of species before the
emergence of humankind (Birch & Cobb 1981, 38, 40). Rather, Life
is exhibited in the continual evolution of new species within and
contributing to a "web of life" constituted by the interdependent relations among all living creatures.

In short, Life is exhibited in the emergence of novel forms of
rich experiences within a finite, interdependent web of mutually sustaining relationships constituted by a diverse but continuous range of
species, from single-cell organisms to human beings. Cobb thus
depicts Life as the source of novelty and as intimately related to all
things. This description recalls Whitehead's dipolar conception of
God, and, in fact, Cobb points out that God as Primordial and
Consequent "is the supreme and perfect exemplification of the ecological model of life" (Birch & Cobb 1981, 195).[4] I take this to
mean that the ecological model points to Life as not only the incarnation of God as Primordial, the principle of creative advance, but
also as Consequent and supremely related to the world. If my observation is accurate, it raises a question about Cobb's identification of
Christ as the incarnation of the Logos or Primordial Nature of God
alone. This question will be discussed below in the section "The
Creative Transformation of Christ." I now turn to the question of
how Christians are to conform to Christ as Life.

A CHRISTIAN ECOLOGICAL ETHIC

Cobb holds that conformation to Christ as Life is fundamentally a "style of life" which grows out of one's experience of Life rather than compliance with specific moral principles or rules of conduct, although—as will be discussed in the next chapter—there are important moral principles that can help guide ethical behavior. Because "human beings are more deeply moved by the way they experience their world than by the claims ethics [i.e., any body of rational moral principles] makes on them" (Birch & Cobb 1981, 176), Cobb believes that moral principles, important as they are, are not sufficient in themselves—"not radical enough"—to bring about the sort of ethics needed to respond adequately to the ecological crisis (Birch & Cobb 1981, 144). Moreover, moral "principles and guidelines [themselves] . . . must be subject to transformation in the continuing process" (Birch & Cobb 1981, 179). Hence, Cobb's ecological ethic is primarily concerned with the formation of a "new consciousness," "sensibility," or style of life rooted in the recognition of Life as the incarnation of God.

Cobb's belief that a new sensibility or style of life is fundamental to a Christian ecological ethics is not surprising in light of the importance that he gives to the character ideal of authentic Christian existence. Consistent with his designation of the structure of Christian existence as the heart of faith, Cobb refers to this sensibility as "faith in Life" (Birch & Cobb 1981, 177 f.). To have faith in Life as the source of all created goods allows us to recognize that "the creative process that brought these goods into being in the past is capable of bringing new goods into being in the future," as well as to recognize that when we devote ourselves to anything less than the creative good we tend to "block the emergence of new goods" (Birch & Cobb 1981, 178). Hence, for Cobb, the style of life which grows out of faith in Life is characterized by trust in and service to Life (Birch & Cobb 1981, 179).

Generally speaking, trust in Life connotes both an openness to Life and a basic confidence that Life works toward an overall increase in richness of experience. Service is active trust: it is cooperation with, "alertly participating" in, and promoting Life's activities. Although *trust* may appear to connote passivity and *service* may appear to connote activity, Cobb does not draw a sharp distinction between the two notions. This is so because Cobb believes that trust requires deliberate and active openness to others while service may often require non-interference in the workings of Life. In short, to trust and serve Life means to attend to and to promote Life's workings.

As noted above, the workings of Life are exhibited in the ecological model of life. Hence, to elucidate in more detail the ethic of trusting and serving Life, it is important to look at what trust and service means in light of the ecological model. For the most part, the ecological model is a translation of Whitehead's organismic view of the world into the language of biology (Birch & Cobb 1981, 8). Hence, Cobb holds that the ecological model, like the organismic world view is illuminative of the level of atoms and electrons (Birch & Cobb 1981, 90), as well as the level of human political society (Birch & Cobb 1981, 273 ff.). However, the ecological model is more explicitly informed by the insights of environmental biology than physics or sociology. Hence, it calls special attention to the relationships among human and subhuman organisms. The scope of this chapter does not permit elaboration of Cobb's and Birch's subtle and detailed derivation of the ecological model of life from a Whiteheadian interpretation of modern biological science. However, it is instructive to examine eight interrelated features of the ecological model which are especially important to an ethic of trust in and service to Life (see Birch & Cobb 1981, 273 f.):

1. *All living things have intrinsic value.* Biology indicates that all living creatures display some form of "taking account of the environment" or subjective experience (Birch & Cobb 1981, 122). The presence of subjective experience in animals indicates that they have immediate enjoyment of their own existence, and hence that they have intrinsic value (Birch & Cobb 1981, 151). This observation supports the Whiteheadian doctrine that all actual occasions experience intrinsic value (cf. Cobb 1965a, 100). Cobb suggests that intrinsic value can be measured in terms of richness of experience, or, put differently, the presence of life, for an individual's capacity for richness of experience is proportionate to its capacity for openness to novelty, and thus to Life. This implies that intrinsic value is variable among different species. Thus, in general, Cobb believes that

presence of intrinsic value increases according to a species' location on the evolutionary ladder.

To recognize the intrinsic value in other living creatures de-objectifies them and forces us to see them as ends in themselves and not simply as things to be manipulated for our own fulfillment or consumption. That is, the creatures of the subhuman world are also ends in themselves, as well as instrumentally valuable to humanity. Hence, "trust in Life leads to [a] shift from control to support in our attitude toward living things. It is a reason for favouring wilderness over wildlife management wherever the choice is possible" (Birch & Cobb 1981, 187). In short, trust in and service to Life encourages an attitude of respect for living things and openness to being shaped by the power of Life itself. As we shall see in the next chapter, Cobb takes this feature to be the basis of rights and justice in our relationship to subhuman species.

2. As members of a web of life, *living individuals are constituted by their relations to each other.* That is to say, "living things behave as they do only in interaction with the other things which constitute their environments" (Birch & Cobb 1981, 83). Moreover, the richness of one's relations contributes to one's richness of experience, which, in turn, "depends upon the richness of what is experienced" (Birch & Cobb 1981, 274). This feature, an example on the level of biology of the Whiteheadian doctrine of internal relations, calls attention to the dependence of each individual upon others in its environment, as well as to the influence of each individual's actions upon the rest of its environment.

This feature of the ecological model directs trust and service toward enhancing the richness of internal relations. This means that we are to become more aware of how we are enriched by all living creatures, including the subhuman world, which, in turn, are affected in their richness of experience by our own decisions and actions. That is, we are to relate to others, human and subhuman, not solely as individuals, but also as fundamentally interconnected with their environment. For example,

> The health of the organism depends on a healthful environment and a healthy life-style that relates the person to the environment. This suggests that primary attention should be directed toward a healthful en-

vironment and healthy behaviour for all rather than to
the manipulation of limited sub-systems [i.e., surgical
and medicinal treatment of symptoms] of the few.
(Birch & Cobb 1981, 207)

Moreover, trusting and serving Life entails promoting Life,
and Life promotes richness of experience. That is, God who is incarnate in Life is internally related to the world, and thus God is enriched by God's experience of the world. Hence, insofar as we promote richness of experience among subhuman and human creatures,
we promote richness of experience in God.

3. Although intimately related to the other individuals in
their environments, *living individuals also transcend their relationships to others* (Birch & Cobb 1981, 274). This feature is a corollary to the understanding of life as the degree of openness to novelty
which results in a greater capacity for self-determination, and thus
transcendence over the causal past. Transcendence is profoundly
dramatized by the way living organisms act as counter-forces to the
basic movement of the universe toward entropy. While the general
tendency of the universe is to decline from a state of greater order and
complexity to a state of lesser order and homogeneity, living
organisms form local pockets of order, growth, and complexity (Birch
& Cobb 1981, 14). The story of the evolution of increasingly more
diverse and complex species is also the story of the emergence of new
capacities for transcendence of life over the forces of entropy.

To trust and serve Life's fight against entropy is to be open
to novelty, and thus to the future. To trust Life is to have hope that
we can transcend the past toward a better future. Cobb notes that "the
novel, unforseeable and uncontrollable possibility is the working of
Life that overcomes the force of entropy. If we trust Life we become
more alive" (Birch & Cobb 1981, 184). To promote openness to
novelty is to promote the conditions for self-determination in oneself
and all other living things because self-determination is concomitant
to the presence of novelty in experience. For this reason, Cobb understands ecological ethics to be an ethics of "the liberation of life."

With respect to the liberation of subhuman life, the evolutionary notion of natural selection has taught us that one of the prime
conditions for the survival and novel development of new species in
the subhuman world is diversity, especially in genetic endowment

(Birch & Cobb 1981, 51 ff.). For example, when we seek to replace a complex ecosystem of plant life with monocultures of hybrid crops, we limit the conditions for novel development which allow the ecosystem to sustain itself in the face of "pests" and weather changes (cf. Birch & Cobb 1981, 302). Hence, to promote conditions which encourage novel development we must ensure—and in some cases reintroduce—diversity among the species that make up our biosphere. In many cases we must simply allow the ecosystem to take care of itself.

Promotion of the conditions of novel development and self-determination has its implications for political liberation as well. Cobb notes that "trust in Life is the advocacy of human freedom. No one can force another human being to be fully open to Life, but on the whole we are most likely to be truly alive when we can participate in the shaping of our own destiny and experience responsibility for one another" (Birch & Cobb 1981, 187). Of course, human beings are more capable of novelty and self-determination than other living things. Indeed, Cobb asserts that "the activity of transcending, which is present in all living things, is dominant in humanity to such an extent that human beings are products more of culture than of biology" (Birch & Cobb 1981, 139). Thus, in Life's struggle against entropy "human life is the fighting frontier of the progressive integration of the universe" (Birch & Cobb 1981, 191 f.). Although Cobb affirms that humanity's capacity for transcendence places it at the top of the evolutionary ladder, a greater capacity for transcendence and self-determination is not so much a privileged position as it is a cosmic responsibility to act as "the shock troops" in the fight against entropy (Birch & Cobb 1981, 192).

It must be noted that the quest for varied, apparently new experiences "for the sake of stimulus and excitement" is not the same as openness to novelty. Rather, this quest "expresses entropy," for there is no emerging synthesis or unity of experience, no integration in an overall satisfaction (Birch & Cobb 1981,185). Without the emergence of new levels of order, mere succession of varied experiences inevitably leads to decline of intensity and richness.[5] Similarly, not all forms of stability and repetitions of past patterns are necessarily entropic; for example, "habit and discipline may either serve Life or oppose it" depending on whether or not they free one "for new processes of creative transformation by Life" (Birch & Cobb

1981, 185). Cobb notes that learning to walk for the first time is an experience of creative transformation. However, if one were to give all one's conscious attention to walking, even as an adult, "life would be thwarted" (Birch & Cobb 1981, 185). Only as walking becomes a habit, freeing one's attention and energy for new possibilities and self-determination, does it serve creative transformation. In short, change and stability serve Life so long as they do not turn past achievements into ends and thus limit the possibility for novel change (Birch & Cobb 1981, 186).

    4. The capacity for novelty is not absolute: there are *limits to transcendence* (Birch & Cobb 1981, 274). This feature reflects the Whiteheadian doctrine that the initial ideal aim at novelty is always relevant to the past of the occasion. Transcendence occurs only in the context of a concrete, conditioned history, that is, in relation to the causal past. Even the ability of humanity to transcend its biological basis through culture does not negate genetic and environmental conditioning (Birch & Cobb 1981, 139). A striking example of the limitation to transcendence can be seen in the limitations that accompany one of the greatest achievements of transcendence in the realm of human thought, namely, the role that political and economic interests play in scientific thought (Birch & Cobb 1981, 281). The ongoing debate among U.S. scientists about the feasibility of President Reagan's "Strategic Defense Initiative" often seems guided more by partisan commitments and the possibility of lucrative defense contracts than by a consideration of objective scientific evidence.

    Trust in and service to Life requires recognition not only of the limits to novel change, but also an awareness of the factors that condition our own thinking and acting. Thus, trust and service call for continual self-criticism. Moreover, to recognize that there are limits to transcendence is to recognize that the subhuman world is not entirely malleable to human endeavors. This leads to the next feature.

    5. The limits to transcendence also apply to the human species in its relationships to other animal species. The evolutionary evidence of continuity between species demonstrates that *there is continuity between humans and other animals.* Although the human species is at the apex of what Aldo Leopold calls the "biotic pyramid" (see Cobb 1972b, 55 f.), its differences from other animal species are

differences of degree. This feature reaffirms the feature of interrelatedness of all creatures and, in Cobb's mind, refutes the dominant anthropocentric interpretation of nature (Birch & Cobb 1981, 282). To recognize the continuity between the human and subhuman world does not so much depreciate human value as it elevates the value of subhuman creatures, although it does mean that the value of human life is not absolute.

However, human beings often do not express trust in Life in light of this feature. Because humanity's ability to transcend is such that we are able to differentiate our own aims at richness of experience from the aims of the strategies of life, we often perceive that differentiation as competition and tend to view ourselves and live as if we were outside of and not limited by the subhuman world. Consequently, we often thwart the strategies of life by viewing the subhuman world as a province to be conquered or escaped from rather than the realm in which we make our home (cf. Birch & Cobb 1981, 262). Trust in Life as the basis of humanity's continuity with the subhuman world means that people should recognize and come to live as though "people are guests on this planet, guests of each other and all other creatures" (Birch & Cobb 1981, 282). Thus, the future of humanity should be seen as intimately bound up with that of the subhuman world.

6. Although the aim of Life at novelty, growth, and richness of experience counters the forces of entropy, *there are limits to the carrying capacity of the planet*. This feature is another important instance of the limits to transcendence. The limits of the planet result from its "limited capacity to produce renewable resources such as timber, food and water, . . . [its] limited amount of non-renewable resources such as fossil fuels and minerals, and . . . [its] limited capacity for providing its free services for the maintenance of the life-systems such as its pollution absorption capacity" (Birch & Cobb 1981, 242). Overpopulation, overconsumption, and pollution have strained our planet's carrying capacity to its limits, that is, they have come close to exhausting the concrete conditions which allow for growth in population, consumption, and disposal of waste.

However, reaching the limits of the planet's carrying capacity does not necessarily entail an end to all growth, but it does require a change in the types of growth that occur so that ecological sustainability rather than economic and population growth becomes our goal. When limits to growth are reached, growth needs to pass into a phase of "maturity" to ensure sustainability. For example, a rain forest is a mature or "steady-state," sustainable ecosystem, which is nevertheless a dynamic society of greatly diverse species that continue to flourish by recycling their resources (Birch & Cobb 1981, 240 f.). Cobb recalls John Stuart Mill's recognition that even when material growth, particularly economic growth, enters into a phase of maturity, it does not negate the possibility of growth in culture, morality, and social progress (Birch & Cobb 1981, 244).

Moreover, there remains an overwhelming need for economic growth among the two-thirds world just to attain the basic necessities of food, shelter, and health care. Hence, Cobb notes that "recognition of the reality of global limits to growth has one obvious and revolutionary corollary. The only way the poor world can grow is for the rich world to curb its own growth" (Birch & Cobb 1981, 262). To trust and serve Life does not preclude sacrifice or even suffering in bringing about the aims of Life. This is not surprising when we realize that to name Christ "Life" is to transform the meaning of Life. In particular, we are called to recognize the relationship of Life to the way of the cross (cf. 1979, 156). In a very real way the cause of Life on our planet calls for a willingness to sacrifice our interests, our comforts, for the sake of the planet. This way of the cross is clearly more appropriate for those of us in the first world than in the two-thirds world. Therefore, among all nations there needs to be an active restructuring of the economy such that the first world moves away from growth so that the two-thirds world can achieve growth.

7. The limited carrying capacity of the planet requires a new vision for a sustainable future, and the possibility of transcendence means that the future is open, but "the ecological model forbids the formulation of a static blueprint for a future Utopia" (Birch & Cobb 1981, 273). In projecting the relationship of humans to each other and to the rest of the world, *there is no single ideal of a future society.* This feature is a corollary to the feature of transcendence. The future is always open-ended and requires re-visioning of all ideals or it becomes entropic. Life is the principle of growth introducing tension between what has been and what might be, continuously challenging and upsetting established ideals while making possible the discovery of new and better ideals. Even a vision of a "steady state" or "no growth" ecosystem cannot preclude novel change. What is best for

our world "is not an ideal state to be attained once for all but a process in which Life is freed to work its creative transformation" (Birch & Cobb 1981, 188).

Moreover, all novel change is attended by ambiguity. Cobb sees this as one of the great insights of Reinhold Niebuhr: the fact that the future is open and in part subject to human decision means that it is as open to the possibility of evil as it is of good. Even evolutionary progress is a paradoxical "fall upward." That is, each new level of transcendence makes possible not only greater potential for richness of experience, but also greater potential to experience pain and suffering (Birch & Cobb 1981, 120). This ambiguity is also reflected in Whitehead's doctrine that all things which come into existence are also subject to "perpetual perishing." Cobb sees this ambiguity as the basic threat to hope for progress (1975, 224). However, Cobb's vision of human and subhuman destiny is not inexorably tragic; he also believes that the strategies of Life give us some reason to trust that there is possibility for some ultimate progress, because in the long view—over the millions of years in which life has emerged and developed—there have been changes which we can call progress (cf. 1981b, 15). Nonetheless, Cobb does *not* believe that hope for a better future is equivalent to assurance that everything will work out. Cobb has no doubt that if humanity continues on its destructive course, humanity will annihilate itself along with most other forms of life on this planet. Hope is a more modest belief that "there are possibilities open in the future that will carry us through the present crisis" (Cobb & Griffin 1976, 156). To trust and serve Life is to seek those possibilities and to recognize the risks of all change. To trust and serve Life is to live responsibly and adventurously.

8. Finally, *conflicting interests and goals among species, and among peoples, which appear competitive or exclusive can become mutually supportive.* This feature of the ecological model mirrors the description of creative transformation as turning conflicting experiences into contrasts which are taken up into a harmonious synthesis. Cobb also refers to this feature as "the possible symbiosis of desirable goals" (Birch & Cobb 1981, 274). Some who interpret evolution as ruthless competition among species in which the the survival of one species requires the extinction of others will argue that the survival and flourishing of humanity inevitably results

in "trade-offs" that bring human gain at subhuman loss. However, although this sort of competition certainly has occurred in the evolution of species, the general trend of evolution is toward a symbiosis of goals or mutual adaptation, so that the survival of one species is actually enhanced by the the survival of others. One can see such evolutionary co-adaptation in the relationship of the Yucca moth and the Yucca flower: the flower's ovules provide an optimum place for the moth to lays its eggs, and the moth's activity of laying eggs provides the flower with the only means to be fertilized (Birch & Cobb 1981, 30 f.).

One apparently irreconcilable conflict between humanity and the subhuman world is the commitment of a large segment of humanity to live in cities which have a deleterious impact on the environment due to the problems of urban sprawl, pollution, and inefficient use of energy. Cobb points to a realistic symbiosis of the commitment to urban living and the need for the environment to go its own way in Paolo Soleri's proposal to build architectural ecologies or "arcologies" (cf. 1975, 195 ff.; Birch & Cobb 1981, 327 f.). Each city would be a three-dimensional structure housing homes, factories, schools, and recreational facilities, rather than a two-dimensional sprawl of separate buildings that are so far apart that large amounts of energy and resources must be expended simply to take care of daily necessities. Arcologies would radically expand upon the architectural trend toward "huge clusters of buildings which combine living and working space with other facilities" so as to become massive organic structures that include living, working, educational, and recreational areas. They would be built to complement the environment

> in such a way that they would make maximum use of the sun's direct energy. They could also be surrounded by greenhouses which would provide food while their sloping roofs would channel heated air into the city. Factories would be located underground, and their waste heat would provide energy for the city. In short a city could be built so that its total energy needs would be a fraction of those of our present cities, and these needs could be met by the sun. (Birch & Cobb 1981, 327)

Trust in and service to Life means that "when confronted by apparently conflicting goods . . . [one ought] to think first about the kinds of changes that would be required so as to make possible the attainment of both" (Birch & Cobb 1981, 285). This attitude makes explicit what has been implicit in several of the other features, for to look for a symbiosis of goals is to recognize that there are possibilities of transcendence while recognizing that transcendence takes place in the context of the given world; and it is to recognize that we are so interrelated that we enrich our own experience when we enrich the experience of others.

These eight features of the ecological model of life help direct trust in and service to Life. However, because Cobb believes that we ought to be attentive to these strategies of life and to promote them where we can, one might be tempted to interpret him as advocating a form of natural law ethics, namely, to act in a manner fitting to the ecological model. Indeed, Cobb does imply that ecological ethics should "conform to reality" (Birch & Cobb 1981, 151). But to interpret Cobb as advocating a natural law ethics obscures the fundamentally dynamic and unpredictable nature of Life. Christians are not only to recognize their interdependence with all living creatures, but they are also to be open to and promote novel change. For Cobb even our judgments of what is good and right are "created goods that need to be transformed continuously by the creative good" (Birch & Cobb 1981, 179). The motive and goal for acting in a manner fitting to the ecological model is to serve Life as creative transformation. But the ecological model is only a model, a "created good," and not meant to be set up as an idol in place of the creative good. Therefore, Cobb is not advocating a new natural law theory, unless it be acknowledged that all natural laws are not only relative, but inevitably subject to creative transformative change.

As noted above, Cobb identifies trusting and serving Life with having religious faith. And because Life for Cobb is Christ, faith in Life is Christian faith. I suggest that the implications of the ecological model for trust in and service to Life also point to two other theological virtues, namely, hope and love. To trust and serve Life's struggle against entropy, and to trust and serve Life's aim at a symbiosis of conflicting goods, is to have hope that the future is not essentially tragic, but that the future is open to genuine progress. However, as was noted above, this hope is not naive confidence. Nor is hope a guarantee that one's present projects will be fulfilled (Birch & Cobb 1981, 182). It recognizes the ambiguity that attends to all creative advance. Even so, the vision of God which exemplifies the ecological model of life indicates a God who is intimately related to the world, who preserves every good in an everlasting synthesis of divine experience (Birch & Cobb 1981, 199).

Moreover, to trust and serve Life is to recognize one's internal relatedness with all other creatures, to allow oneself to be constituted by those relationships, and to promote future richness of experience in others. Put differently, to trust and serve Life is to be open to the entire past and the entire future, that is, it is to love all things (cf. above). To fully trust and serve Life is to love all creatures because

> Life is the supreme instance of *love*. ... Life favours all living things, and precisely for that reason does not take sides in our inevitably competitive existence. ... This love that is the most intimate and particular of all loves, is at the same time awesomely disinterested and, in that sense, impersonal. For Jesus, too, the perfect love of the personal God is manifest in this: that the sun shines on just and unjust alike. (Birch & Cobb 1981, 198)

Hence, the ecological model helps to make explicit what was implicit in Cobb's initial revision of his christocentric ethic, namely, that the ideal of Christian love extends to all creatures, human and subhuman. However, Cobb is not advocating an undifferentiated reverence for life, counting every creature as having the same value. Rather, Cobb suggests there are appropriate expressions of reverence or respect for different forms of life (Birch & Cobb 1981, 149). I will return to this issue in the next chapter.

CONCLUSIONS

TRANSFORMATION OF METHOD

Before turning to a more detailed elaboration of Cobb's post-1969 social ethics in chapters four and five, it is appropriate to note the transformation of Cobb's theological method that accompanies the transformation of his christology and ethics. Cobb's pre-1969 method grows out of response to the "fundamental religious problem" of doubt as the obstacle to faith. In other words, the problem for method was primarily *intellectual* and *existential*. To that end, Cobb primarily sought to find what is unique and superior about Christian faith. However, the ecological crisis introduces a new problem for theological method, especially insofar as Christian theology has contributed to the ethos or world view undergirding the ecological crisis. In order to overcome doubt, Cobb's pre-1969 method attempted to identify the existential essence of Christian faith that was more primitive than any beliefs or doctrines, namely, the Christian structure of existence. Cobb notes that this method was "reductionistic" in its search for a single, unique essence of Christianity (see 1975, 27, esp. n. 7). Moreover, he recognizes that his pre-1969 formulation of the structure of Christian existence was "exclusivistic" in its assumption that Christian existence was unique and final in relation to all other forms of existence. At best, he thought that one could choose between competing forms of existence, that is, between competing Ways (see 1981a, 78).

With his recognition of the imminence of world-wide ecological disaster, Cobb realizes that the adequacy of the Christian structure of existence, much less any claims it might have to finality, is radically called into question, because Christian existence as self-transcending selfhood has contributed to the technological and socio-economic world view responsible for today's ecological crisis. Moreover, at the same time, Cobb has come to realize that any exclusivistic claim for the finality of Christian faith is further discredited by the reality of pluralism—religious, political, and moral (1975, 18). Consequently, Cobb recognizes a new challenge to Christian faith which is more than intellectual or existential. This challenge is posed by our inability to cooperate with each other on this planet to provide a creative, hopeful vision for survival (cf. 1975, 22). Thus, Cobb no longer sees intellectual and existential doubt as the primary obstacles to faith; rather, the lack of a collective, hopeful vision as an alternative to the technological and socio-economic world view which underlies the impetus toward ecological catastrophe is the fundamental obstacle to Christian faith. Hence, Cobb comes less to see theological method as providing a merely intellectual expression consistent with the original witness of

Christian faith, than with providing a creative moral and religious vision that promises hope in Christ. In *Christ in a Pluralistic Age* Cobb refers to the change in his method as a shift from a "modernist" to a "post-modern pluralistic" method (1975, 15).

An important feature of Cobb's post-modern pluralistic method is his rejection of the academic disciplinarian approach to Christian theology. Indeed, it is somewhat unfair to imply that Cobb has a specifiable method because in many ways he has renounced the centrality of the question of theological method as an abstraction from concrete thinking about fundamental crises affecting Christians. Cobb states,

> I have concluded that insofar as "theology" is the name of an academic discipline (*Wissenschaft*) confined to a particular method and subject matter, it is not worthy of the amount of attention it receives. ... What I do feel called to do is to think, self-consciously as a Christian, about those important questions to whose answering I have reason to hope I can make some contribution. (1985d, 1)

Disciplinary thinking is based upon an Enlightenment atomistic-substantialist model of reality. Such a reality has no center, only independent, circumscribed spheres, knowable by independent disciplines having appropriate methods designed to answer appropriate questions. Cobb recognizes that the magnitude of the ecological question confounds a disciplinary answer, for the ecological crisis cuts across theological, moral, social, psychological, biological, economic, and geo-political realms.

The disciplinarian distinctions that inhibit an adequate understanding and response to the crucial questions confronting our planet are insidiously manifest in the traditional separation of the discipline of theology from the discipline of ethics. Cobb confesses that for a long time he assumed that the sphere of ethics is concerned with different questions than the sphere of systematic theology, even though he has

> never been personally indifferent to human suffering and injustice. ... But for many years I thought that Christian reflection on the questions of the relief of

suffering and oppression belonged to the discipline of theological ethics and not to that of systematic theology. It took years of buffeting by black theology, liberation theology, political theology, and feminism before I was fully aware of the seriousness of this distortion. But I do now understand that oppression is a theological problem as much as an ethical one—or, more accurately, that this distinction of theology and ethics is a disastrous part of the heritage of the disciplinary organization of thought, one by which I myself had been particularly victimized. (1985d, 18)

Cobb's shift to christocentrism completes his turn away from specifically methodological questions toward what he calls "global Christian thinking" (1985d, 1). Global Christian thinking requires one "to understand all things in relation to Christ . . . [to] seek an understanding of the true nature of all things as a Christian" (1985d, 10). Put differently, global Christian thinking is "holistic thinking" (1981a, 77), that recognizes that "all events are constituted by their relations and these relations cut across the artificial disciplinary boundaries" (1985d, 16). Cobb concludes that for the Christian, "the ecological reality should be reflected in the structures of thought and investigation" (1985d, 16). Hence, insofar as Cobb's global Christian thinking can be called a new method, it is a christocentric, ecological method.

In spite of the profound shift in Cobb's method, there is significant continuity with his early method, especially the conspicuous role that speculation, specifically, Whiteheadian cosmology, continues to play. This continuity is illustrated by Cobb's reappropriation of the Whiteheadian doctrine of the subjectivity of all living things to extend the interpretation of love to the subhuman world. If anything, the role of Whitehead's cosmology plays perhaps a more prominent role in Cobb's post-1969 thought. For example, in his early ethics, Cobb does not even discuss "perpetual perishing," much less associate it with evil; whereas, in his discussion of the ambiguities of progress, alluded to above, Cobb states that these ambiguities—of the possibilities of evil accompanying every achievement of good—"are rooted in time . . . [as] perpetual perishing" (1975, 224). Hence, Cobb affirms that in his efforts to respond to the ecological crisis, he has become "more of a Whiteheadian than before" because Whitehead contains "the sensitivities called for in the new situation" (1981a, 77).

It may seem that the importance that Cobb gives to Whitehead in his post-1969 theology has changed his method from a *Christian* natural theology to a natural theology, and hence, Tracy and Ogden have been vindicated in their claim that Cobb is simply seeking to ground Christian beliefs in a Whiteheadian cosmology. However, even though it is true that Cobb is even more self-consciously Whiteheadian, it must be noted that Cobb recognizes that Whitehead's cosmology is "incomplete" and only a "model of reality" which he believes is better than the atomistic-substantialist model that often remains presupposed and unexamined in much of Christian theology (1985d, 11). Thus, Cobb does not view Whitehead's thought as a new sort of scholastic philosophy. Moreover, Cobb argues that he does not subordinate the Christian faith and the Bible to an "alien" world view, for not only is Whitehead's thought profoundly influenced by a christological vision, as Altizer points out, but there is

> no one who does not think and interpret the Bible in terms of some notion about reality, consciously or not. Most, today, are deeply influenced by the [atomistic and substantialist] Enlightenment model, even if—indeed especially if—they have never thought much about it. This model is deeply antithetical to the Biblical world view and has seriously weakened our living relation to the Bible, whereas Whitehead's model is far more continuous and congenial. (1985d, 16 f.)

In fact, Cobb's method is certainly more deeply centered on Christ than his earlier method. Of course, Cobb's understanding of Christ and the role of Christ in theological method is still far from that of a Karl Barth, in part because it is profoundly influenced by the ecological or Whiteheadian world view. Nonetheless, Cobb's understanding of the ecological world view is also profoundly influenced by Christ as revealed in Jesus of Nazareth. Cobb understands himself as reflecting upon the crucial questions of our time *as* a Christian thinker, that is, as one "whose identity is constituted by the memory [of Jesus of Nazareth] that the church celebrates" (1985d, 28).

Just as important, the danger of speculation—which Cobb continues to recognize—seems to be countered in part by the self-critical attitude demanded by his christocentricity. Put differently, theological method or Christian global reflection itself must be subject to creative transformation—to Christ—since it is also a created good. Hence, I suggest that another way of referring to Christian global thinking is in terms of "theological method as creative transformation."

Like his early theological method, Cobb's understanding of Christian global thinking retains a commitment to empirical knowledge and experience. Not only does Cobb believe that Whitehead's cosmology is incomplete and in need of integration with new advances in knowledge (1985d, 11), he also draws upon the insights of biology and other sciences to inform the ecological model. Moreover, as noted above, Cobb has taken over much of Wieman's empirical analysis of the creative good into his understanding of Christ as creative transformation, while prevailing upon speculation to offer a correction of the ontological deficiencies in Wieman's analysis.

Given the centrality of Christ, the prominence of Whiteheadian cosmology, and the importance of Wieman's empirical analysis to Cobb's understanding of Christ, it seems fair to say that Cobb's post-1969 method goes even further than his early method in combining neo-orthodox, rationalist, and empirical insights into a theological method which takes seriously the central insights of each. Hence, Cobb both continues and transforms his early empirical method. Moreover, Cobb's theological method of creative transformation has an important implication for his christology, namely, that christology must also be subject to creative transformation.

THE CREATIVE TRANSFORMATION OF CHRIST

Christ as creative transformation is for Cobb an image that is also subject to creative transformation. Cobb observes that "any attempt to fix the meaning of 'Christ' is doomed to arbitrariness and artificiality. ... 'Christ' is a living symbol, not a proper name or common noun" (1987, 1). Hence, Cobb continues to reassess and revise his christology in light of the insights and criticism of Buddhism, liberation theology, and feminism. The transformation of

Cobb's christology is perhaps best illustrated by his encounter with Latin American and feminist liberation theologies.

For some time Cobb has understood Christ as creative transformation to be exemplified by "conscientization," Paulo Freire's method for educating the oppressed which has become central to the theological method of Latin American liberation theology (1987, 15). As Cobb understands Freire, conscientization, like creative transformation, incarnates the activity of the Logos—God's Primordial Nature—by stressing the possibility of transcending inherited patterns of thinking and living by creating a new critical consciousness. However, Latin American liberation theologians have also argued that Christ is present in the poor. Thus, while Cobb's christology identifies Christ as creative transformation with conscientization, Latin American liberation christology identifies Christ with the poor and oppressed. Cobb recognizes that this difference raises a problem for his own understanding of conscientization, and hence, for his view of Christ.

> To call this conscientization Christianization is to imply that the poor are not Christian until they are conscientized. ... The association of creative transformation with the transformation of thought and of culture can lead—indeed it has led—to locating Christ primarily among the cultural and intellectual elite. (1987, 15-15a)

Without giving up his identification of Christ with the Primordial Nature of God, Cobb examines the possibility of incorporating the notion that Christ is present in the poor by reinterpreting Christ as creative transformation as the incarnation of both the Primordial and Consequent Natures of God. This revision represents a shift in Cobb's christology. Indeed, Cobb acknowledges that until recently he avoided viewing Christ as the incarnation of God's Consequent Nature, in large part because he identifies God's Consequent Nature with the Holy Spirit; whereas traditional theological doctrine holds that Christ is only the incarnation of the Logos, which for Cobb is the Primordial Nature of God. Thus, Cobb tried to stay within the boundaries of the traditional doctrine that Christ is the incarnation of the Logos, but not of the Holy Spirit

(1985d, 20-22; 1987, 17). However, Cobb's encounter with Latin American liberation theology has led him to question (a) whether his adherence to this traditional doctrine is as true to the biblical experience as is the belief that Christ is present in the poor and oppressed; (b) whether the traditional doctrine itself is consistent with belief in the unity of the Trinity; as well as (c) whether his adherence to this doctrine is an obstacle to a fuller experience of creative transformation, and thus, to Christian faith.

Consequently, Cobb has come to the conclusions: (a) that the Latin American experience of Christ's presence in the poor and oppressed faithfully reflects the biblical experience expressed in I Corinthians 1:18-31, which states that Christ is made known in the foolishness of this world; (b) that to suggest that Christ is not also the incarnation of the Holy Spirit creates an exception to the traditional teaching on the unity of the Trinity, namely, that all persons of the Trinity co-act; and, most importantly, (c) that faithfulness to the doctrine that Christ is only the incarnation of the Logos can pose an obstacle to being transformed by Latin American Liberation theology's insight that Christ is known in the poor and oppressed (1985d, 20 f.). Indeed, Latin American liberation theology's

> identification of Christ with the poor has important advantages. To locate Christ fully in and with the poor does justice to Jesus' belief that what we do to the least we do to "the Son of Man." It points out the error of our overwhelming tendency to think that the "successful" are of more importance and worth. It shows that we should measure the real effectiveness of our policies by their effects upon the "least." It also teaches us to listen to the poor. ... If Christ is identified with the poor, then to hear the poor is to hear the voice of Christ. (1987, 15 f.)

Hence, Cobb concludes that "Christ is not only the way God is in the world [through the Logos] but also the way the world is in God" (1987, 17). That is, Christ is not only the incarnation of God's Primordial Nature, but also God's Consequent Nature.

That Christ incarnates God's experience of the world, means that Christ incarnates the God who "suffers with us in our suffering and rejoices with us in our joy" (1987, 17). To conform to Christ therefore includes sharing the burdens and joys of others. This transformation of the meaning of Christ reinforces the ideal of Christian love as both *agape* and compassion. To a degree, compassion—the constitution of one's present experience by others' experiences—can be understood from the perspective of the incarnation of the Primordial Nature of God in Christ, which is the initial ideal aim that makes possible a greater inclusion of the past by introducing novel possibilities into the present. Put differently, the introduction of novelty, through the agency of God's Primordial Nature, allows for greater synthesis of past experiences; and since the experience of another's experience (empathy) is by definition the experience of the past, conformity to the initial ideal aim furthers one's capacity for compassion. But, when one speaks of the compassion of Christ, one is speaking primarily of Christ's identification with and acceptance of others as they are, rather than how they can be changed. Compassion as understood from the standpoint of the incarnation of the Logos or Primordial Nature of God tends to view compassion instrumentally in the service of transformation; whereas compassion understood from the standpoint of the incarnation of the Consequent Nature of God tends to view compassion as intrinsically important and efficacious. Hence, conformity to Christ as the incarnation of God's Primordial *and* Consequent Natures, lifts up more forcefully Cobb's ideal of Christian love as both *agape* and empathy.

Feminist thinkers have posed a further challenge to the possibility of providing an adequate christology by their observation that Christianity is innately and irrevocably patriarchal because Christ is male (cf. Daly 1977, 84 ff.). However, because the meaning of Christ is transformed to include Christ as the incarnation of God's Consequent Nature, Cobb is able to move beyond the notion of Christ as *Logos*, a masculine noun, to affirm Christ as *Sophia*, a feminine noun which connotes the Wisdom of God who intimately knows the world (1987, 22; cf. I Cor. 1:24). Cobb suggests that *Sophia* captures more fully both the meaning of John the evangelist's *Logos* and Christ's compassionate identification with the oppressed. Hence, Cobb proposes a transformation of the image of Christ "in which Christ names *Sophia* as she embodies herself in the world and receives the world into herself" (1987, 22b).

It should be noted that the transformation of Cobb's christology which comes out of his encounter with Latin American and feminist liberation theologies helps to resolve some inconsistencies revealed earlier in this analysis. I suggested above that Cobb's elucidation of Christ as Life raises a question about the coherence of Cobb's identification of Christ as the incarnation of the Logos or Primordial Nature of God alone, that is, as incarnation of the initial ideal aim given by God. The ecological model of life implies that Christ is supremely related to the world, and thus incarnates God's Consequent Nature. Moreover, Cobb's identification of Christ with the initial ideal aim is not fully consistent with Cobb's earlier form-ulation of the nature of the initial ideal aim in *A Christian Natural Theology*—a formulation that he has never, to my knowledge, changed. In *A Christian Natural Theology* Cobb revises Whitehead to include the role of God's Consequent Nature; yet, Cobb's account of Christ as Logos only identifies Christ, the initial ideal aim, with the Primordial Nature of God. Hence, consistency would imply that if Christ is the incarnation of the initial ideal aim, that would include God as Consequent.

It may seem that, in spite of Cobb's openness to the creative transformation of his own thought by Latin American and feminist liberation theologies, the centrality of his concern with the ecological crisis makes him vulnerable to criticisms from political and lib-eration theologians who perceive this concern for the environment as a first-world, middle-class luxury which neglects the problems of rights, social justice, and socio-political change. However, Cobb's interest in the ecological crisis does not close him off from such human social ethical issues. In fact, for Cobb, the ecological crisis seems to have opened up new dimensions of these issues. Hence, I turn to the implications of Cobb's ecological ethics for human justice and liberation.

NOTES

1. Cobb notes that there have been some Christians whose structure of existence has developed in another direction. A significant, though "subdominant," development of Christian existence is represented by Francis of Assisi and Albert Schweitzer whose high valuation of human life was extended to subhuman life as a "disinterested love of nature" (1972b, 51). However, Cobb does not analyze how disinterested love of nature can develop out of self-transcending selfhood except to say

that concern for others comes to include all creatures (1972b, 51). Given the anomalous character of this development of Christian existence, I question whether it is a subdominant development of self-transcending selfhood so much as a development beyond self-transcending selfhood.

2. There is some controversy in Biblical studies today that John's use of *logos* is rooted in Hebrew usage rather than Greek usage, and therefore is not meant to connote the Greek notion of *Word*. Needless to say, Cobb here is following the traditional interpretation of *logos* as Word.

3. The identification of agape with active goodwill actually comes from Griffin's contribution to *Process Theology: An Introductory Exposition*, co-authored with Cobb. However, in the introduction to that work the authors note that "each has revised the work of the other" and that they "consider the whole their joint project" (Cobb & Griffin 1976, 11). Hence, I employ Griffin's analysis of agape in elucidating Cobb's understanding of love.

4. At first glance, it may appear that Cobb's statement, that God is the supreme exemplification of Life—which has already been identified with Christ—is in danger of falling into the very trap of confusing God with Christ that Cobb was trying to avoid with his earlier christology. This confusion is compounded by the fact that in *The Liberation of Life* (Birch & Cobb, 1981) Cobb refers to Life as God (195), but in "Theology: From Enlightenment Discipline to Global Christian Thinking" (1985d) Cobb states unequivocally that in *The Liberation of Life* what he refers to as Life is Christ (1985d, 24). I have tried to resolve this confusion by taking Cobb's latter statement as authoritative, not only because it is a more recent statement, but also because Cobb does acknowledge in *The Liberation of Life* both that "the *symbol* 'Life' names God in a way that does not highlight the fullness of God's personal being or redemptive action" (Birch & Cobb 1981, 198, italics added), and, as I have noted above, that Life is an "image" of the divine (Birch & Cobb 1981, 199). Hence, I interpret Cobb's statement "Life is God" as "Life is an image of God"—which is consistent with Cobb's assertion that Life refers to Christ.

5. I would question whether the quest for "one new experience after another" is really a quest for novelty at all. The example that comes to mind is that of experimentation with drugs, especially stimulants and hallucinogens. Experimenters often assert that they are seeking

"new" highs.   However, as recent studies in cocaine usage indicate, it may not be a novel high that they are seeking as much as it is the repetition of the first time "rush."   If this is true of other drugs, much of what drug users pass off as seeking new experiences may disguise an actual quest for returning to the past, and would therefore be an expression of entropy.   It may be that such an analysis would hold for other so-called quests for new experiences, e.g., in sexual infidelity or promiscuity, or in consumerism with its insatiable lust for "new" products.

CHAPTER FOUR

FROM ECOLOGY TO SOCIAL JUSTICE: THE POSSIBILITY AND MEANING OF RIGHTS AND JUSTICE

In the previous chapter, I interpreted Cobb's post-1969 ethics as fundamentally a christocentric, ecological ethics, both in form and in substance. In form, because the central normative category for Cobb's post-1969 ethics, Christ as creative transformation is exemplified in the ecological model of life, so that Cobb identifies Christ with Life. In substance, because Cobb believes that *the* most immediate and overwhelming ethical and theological issue confronting humanity is our relationship to the subhuman world. In addition, I noted that Cobb's transformed theological ethics, like his early ethics, emphasizes the formation of a new character or disposition over adherence to principles of conduct or obedience to universal laws.

The ecological form and substance of Cobb's ethics together with its emphasis upon the formation of a disposition of conformation to Christ raise some questions as to whether the aim of Cobb's ethics is in conflict with the aims of traditional approaches to social justice, on the one hand, and with more recent political and liberation theologies, on the other. More specifically, the question is, can an ecological ethics which is primarily concerned with preserving and promoting the organic interrelatedness of all creatures, and which emphasizes the formation of a new structure of character as a fundamental element of the solution to the world's crises, provide or incorporate a theory of human rights, justice, and liberation?

115

From the perspective of traditional social ethics, some critics, such as Max Stackhouse, have questioned process theology's ability to speak adequately to human rights and justice, arguing that "process thought, whatever its other virtues, has not yet given fundamental, positive guides to political life. The question is whether it is constitutionally capable of giving such guidance" (Stackhouse 1981, 105). From the perspective of liberation theology it can be argued that, even if Cobb's process theology is able to provide a grounding for a theory of rights and justice, Cobb's emphasis upon issues of ecology undercuts attention to the urgent issues of human liberation and betokens the concerns of bourgeois, white, North American males rather than the non-white, two-thirds world and women who have to deal first with liberation from political, economic, racial, and sexual oppression before they can worry about the welfare of plants and animals.

It may be an open question whether an adequate social ethics must provide a theory of rights and justice—notions which are typically Western, and more often than not individualistic—or whether it must give central attention to human liberation. Nonetheless, Cobb takes these issues seriously and believes that his ecological model does imply both a solid grounding for rights and justice and a viable understanding of human liberation (see Birch & Cobb 1981, chaps. 5, 8; Cobb 1982b). Hence, the purpose of this chapter and the next is two-fold: (a) to raise and examine what I take to be important criticisms of the ability of John Cobb's process theological ethics to address adequately traditional and modern issues central to social ethics, namely, rights and justice (chapter four), and political and economic liberation (chapter five); and (b) to elaborate Cobb's constructive views on these issues. This chapter looks in-depth at the question of whether (and how) Cobb's ecological ethics can ground the principles of rights and justice.

In order to evaluate and explicate Cobb's view of rights and justice, I will examine what might be called "common sense" objections underlying criticisms by Stackhouse and other social ethicists as to the possibility that a philosophical theology which emphasizes change and process can formulate any strict principles such as rights and justice. The first section presents a cursory sketch of the common elements or requirements of rights and justice. Accepting these requirements as, for the most part, valid, it critically examines and refutes the apparent common sense arguments against process thought's ability to provide a theory of rights and justice.[1] The second section elucidates how Cobb's view of rights and justice fulfills the basic criteria of rights and justice.

The next chapter discusses Cobb's attempt to deal with the issues of political and economic liberation from the perspective of an ecological ethic.

THE CHALLENGE TO PROCESS THOUGHT

In spite of the differences among leading views of justice, from natural law theories to John Rawls' theory of procedural justice, there appears to be a relative consensus that, at the heart of justice, there are two presuppositions: that there are certain limits as to what can be justifiably done to another (and hence of what can be claimed by another); and that there is some standard or standards—such as natural law or a just procedure—by which competing claims can be adjudicated[2] Hence, the concept of justice presupposes that there are certain individual rights which cannot be overridden by others, even for the welfare of society as a whole. At the core of these inviolable individual rights is personal dignity or respect for individuals, that is, recognition of the freedom or ability of individual persons to achieve their rightful interests. Moreover, the notion of a standard by which competing claims can be adjudicated presupposes some determinate ideal or "transcendent structure of reality" which provides critical transcendence for evaluating the status quo, that is, for determining whether present and proposed institutions and practices are just (Stackhouse 1981, 109).[3]

It seems reasonable to me that any adequate theory of justice requires some account of personal dignity as a basis for inviolability or individual rights, and a determinate ideal or "transcendent structure of reality" for evaluating what is and what can be. The question facing process theology in general, and Cobb's ethics in particular, is whether the categories of process thought are able to provide either a basis for affirming individual rights and a context invariant ideal which can offer a transcendent standpoint from which to critique the status quo.

Central to Cobb's theological ethics are the Whiteheadian categories of interrelatedness, creative synthesis, and richness of experience or aesthetic satisfaction. These categories are reflected in the ecological model of life which affirms that all living individuals are constituted by their relations to each other, that living creatures are capable of transcending the given past through novel development, and that the presence of life reflects the presence richness of experience. However, if principles of rights and justice presuppose the inviolability of individuals and an unchanging standard or ideal by which to measure what is due to each person, then common sense would suggest that justice is fundamentally contrary to process theology's understanding of actual entities as organically interrelated, subject to creative advance, and perpetually in pursuit of increasing richness of experience (see Stackhouse 1981; Clark 1981). In short, there appear to be three major problems with a process grounding for justice. First, the essential organic interrelatedness of all individuals appears to contradict the presupposition of justice that individual persons have inviolable limits. Second, the process view that the world is in each moment undergoing creative advance or creative synthesis[4] appears to lead to the conclusion that any given order (social, political, economic, and even personal) is continually being relativized and dissolved, so that, in principle, there is no possibility of right order. Finally, if the process view of the aim at value as richness of experience or aesthetic satisfaction is the basis for determining the "rightful interests" of individuals, then there appears to be no point of critical transcendence that would allow a way to distinguish among the relative values of aesthetic achievement—the intensity of a wealthy philanthropist's experience may be no greater than the intensity of torturer's experience (cf. Clark 1981, 136). Let us examine these three problems in detail.

CRITIQUE OF INTERRELATEDNESS

On the surface, it seems that the importance placed by process thinkers on internal relatedness is inimical to personal inviolability in two ways: (a) the view that an occasion of experience is the creative synthesis of its relations and not an enduring substance (or does not at least possess a fixed nature) undermines the notion of individual personhood; and (b) the fact of organic relatedness alone is at best morally neutral and thus "fails to provide guidance relative to the quality of relationships" (Clark 1981, 135).

In the first instance, process thought appears to be "perched precariously on [the] cliff" of "tautological collapse" since if the self or person is defined as constituted by its relations (such as political society), then it would seem difficult to speak of the rights of an individual vis à vis the society to which a person belongs—a society which is largely constitutive of a person (Clark 1981, 136). As Stackhouse puts it, common sense suggests that

> there is a "thingness" about life that does not easily dissolve into its relationships; there is a reality about a self—a Socrates or Jesus, a John Smith or Jane Doe—that is not easily accounted for by appealing to a "synthesis of a multiplicity of relata."
> (1981, 108)

Hence, without some essential or underlying nature or unifying purpose, the self seems to dissolve into a conglomeration of perpetually concrescing experiences without unity and identity, and thus without rights.[5]

In the second instance, the emphasis upon interrelatedness provides no positive moral standard. It would be a mistake to assume that interrelatedness is good or just in itself. Indeed, some relationships are down right evil:

> Relatedness [can take] the form of paternalism, manipulation, oppression and persecution as often as respectfulness, liberation, love or just treatment. Relatedness in fact becomes antithetical to justice if it submerges the reality of an enduring individual person focused in its own right as an irreducible center of irreplaceable worth and dignity. (Clark 1981, 136)

Simply put, the question of which relations are good or just cannot be resolved by an appeal to interrelatedness, but requires some other standard beyond interrelatedness.

The common sense criticism that the process view of the essential interrelatedness of the self dissolves the unity of the self can be answered by reviewing Cobb's understanding of the soul. The unity of a living soul, such as a human self, although not absolute—

amnesia and multiple personalities are common examples of a breakdown in personal unity—is represented by the soul's "peculiar richness of inheritance" of the character of previous occasions of the soul (Whitehead 1978, 109). As pointed out in chapter two, Cobb notes that the soul's personal identity can range from little more than repetitions of past occasions in a serial order—a function of physical prehensions of contiguous events in the mode of causal efficacy—to a "peculiar completeness of summing up" of the past while contributing its own novelty to "the flashes of novelty that have occurred in the past" (see 1965a, 51). What distinguishes the unity of the human soul is the presence of both a high degree of order *and* a high degree of originality. That is, the order of the human person is not simply the repetition of past characteristics as critics seem to suggest; rather, it is the integration of these past characteristics with novel possibilities in a creative synthesis. And, as has been pointed out earlier, the increased presence of novelty allows for a wider, more complex synthesis of feeling, so that novelty makes possible the positive prehension of more past actualities into a greater unity of feeling, and thus greater interrelatedness.

Moreover, common observation seems to indicate that the unity and identity associated with things which are relatively limited in their relations is deficient compared to things which are quite vulnerable to being affected by their relations. For example, empirically speaking, a block of granite, which is nearly impervious to all but a narrow range of relations, has a sort of enduring identity over time, but it has little of the identity and unity associated with our common experience of selfhood. A human being, which is quite vulnerable to more vast and complex relations and changes, is capable of maintaining great unity and identity of self, without resorting to isolation and inflexibility. For process thought this difference lies in the extremely limited and repetitious prehensions that constitute the becoming order of enduring objects which constitute a block of granite compared to that of the enduring objects which constitute a human person. A block of granite has no presiding ordered experience coordinating the enduring objects which constitute it; whereas a human being has a soul, a presiding order of living occasions which forms "the final node, or intersection, of a complex structure of many enduring objects," coordinating the enduring objects which make up the person (Whitehead 1978, 109). Although the identity of a human being is certainly more dynamic and malleable than the identity of a rock, it is hardly without unity. In contrast, the sort of determinate identity implied by Stackhouse's view of a self that "is not easily accounted for by appealing to a 'synthesis of a multiplicity of relata'" appears more akin to the repetitious, monolithic order found in a block of granite than in the vital, multi-faceted order of a human being.

A process understanding of the interrelatedness of the individual, then, does not contradict the unity and identity of the self, and therefore, does not undermine the notion of the person as the locus of rights. Of course, to account for the personal unity of an essentially changing, interrelated self does not provide a normative theory of personal dignity, that is, of a person as an end in herself. This observation raises the second common sense criticism of process thought's emphasis on the category of interrelatedness: that interrelatedness, of itself, provides no principles governing the quality of relationships. Just as psychological egoism is often taken to be the theoretical basis of ethical egoism, process thought's emphasis upon interrelatedness often appears to come across as a normative ideal to be achieved rather than a descriptive account of the world, as if recognition of the interrelatedness of all creatures were sufficient to produce social solidarity and overcome alienation. For example, Douglas Sturm in his analysis of socio-economic alienation draws upon Whitehead's understanding of internal relations to argue that

> Alienation in Marx's understanding is the kind of contradiction between appearance and reality that is particularly characteristic of relations in the capitalist epoch. ... [I]t is a dissimulation of those relations that constitute the species-being of humanity, cast in the language of separation. (Sturm 1981, 94)

The apparent implication of Sturm's position is that conformity to the "reality" of the fundamental interrelatedness of all occasions of experience entails a political theory of "communitarianism" (1981, 99). As critics are quick to point out, such an appeal to the category of relatedness is uncomfortably close to succumbing to the is/ought fallacy. To put it forcefully, "it is the nature, not the fact, of relatedness which is all important for justice. The possibilities of self-contempt and self-respect, dependent as they are on distinctions of right and wrong, noble and base, etc., are not addressed by relatedness or sociality *per se*" (Clark 1981, 136).

I think this criticism is valid, but misleading. It is valid because the category of relatedness does not provide implicit or explicit norms governing *how* relationships should be incorporated into one's synthesis of experience. Without a doubt there are improper and proper forms of relatedness—acts of "paternalism, manipulation, oppression, and persecution" should not be considered as valuable or right as acts of "respectfulness, liberation, love, or just treatment" (Clark 1981, 136). Nevertheless, it is worth noting that those who relate themselves to another as oppressors and manipulators often are acting as though they were not internally related to the other, as though the other were not also a subject of experiencing, and as though their own experience were not somehow affected by the pain and suffering they inflict.

The criticism is misleading because it assumes that for all process thinkers the notion of internal relations is by definition good. For example, Sturm does not state that alienation is a violation of the principle of internal relations—which would imply that the principle of internal relations operates normatively—but is actually an "expression" of the principle (1981, 82, 92). Thus, Sturm takes Marx's theory of alienation as normative, but finds cosmological grounding for Marx's theory in Whitehead's doctrine of internal relations. Moreover, Whitehead explicitly acknowledges that

> apart from some notion of imposed Law, the doctrine of immanence [or internal relations] provides absolutely no reason why the universe should not be steadily relapsing into lawless chaos. In fact, the Universe, as understood in accordance with the doctrine of Immanence, should exhibit itself as including a stable actuality whose mutual implication with the remainder of things secures an inevitable trend towards order. The Platonic 'persuasion' is required. (1933, 115)

That is, Whitehead agrees that the cosmological category of interrelatedness cannot provide moral norms, but must be complemented by an account of God as the cosmological principle of order or principle of limitation (see 1925, 178 f.).

However, even though process thinkers admit that awareness of our internal relatedness to others may not provide any norms for *how* we should be related, that awareness does make us more sensitive to the fact that all our actions affect others. Put differently, to recognize that we are "members one of another" does lead us to recognize that "our individual happiness is bound up with the happiness of others" (Birch & Cobb 1981, 278). For process thought the real value of relatedness lies in its being a basis for greater richness of experience and creative advance. This leads us to criticisms of the category of creative synthesis.

CRITIQUE OF CREATIVE SYNTHESIS

The common sense criticisms of the category of creative synthesis or creative advance as incapable of providing any norms for grounding rights and justice are of particular interest for evaluating Cobb's ethics. As we have seen, Christ understood as creative transformation is the central normative category of Cobb's mature theological ethics—and creative transformation can be understood as the exemplification in reality of the metaphysical principle of creative advance (cf. Whitehead 1978, 188, 344; Cobb 1975, 70 ff.).

For Whitehead creativity is the principle of novelty, and thereby "is the ultimate principle by which the many which are the universe disjunctively, become the one actual occasion, which is the universe conjunctively" (Whitehead 1978, 21). Creative advance or creative synthesis is the underlying principle of the concresence of each actual occasion in its self-determination of novel togetherness (1978, 21). Creative synthesis, then, is manifested in the self-determination or self-creation of a concrescing occasion which issues in the emergence of a novel occasion of experience. The metaphysical ultimacy of the principle of creative synthesis has led some critics to conclude that process thought holds that the exercise of freedom in the quest for novelty as the ultimate good (see Clark 1981, 137). Hence, criticisms of the ability of creative synthesis to provide any grounding for rights and justice center around the appropriateness of looking to either novelty or freedom as moral norms.

The problem with novelty as a moral norm, and thus as a basis for right order, is twofold: (a) by virtue of the fact that concrescence is always the "production of novel togetherness" or creativity, every actual occasion is the outcome of some advance into novelty, and therefore, everything that comes to be appears to be just or good (cf. Whitehead 1978, 21); (b) the moral ideal would seem to be the pursuit of novelty for novelty's sake or change for change's sake. In the first case, right order is meaningless as a norm since any order is "right" by virtue of being. In the second case, right order is undermined by "a boundless, unlimited search for new perfection [which] undercuts" any "foundation of self-restraint" or inviolability (Clark 1981, 137).

The problem with freedom or autonomy as a basis for right order is that it appears to devolve into arbitrariness. Critics are correct in their assessment that for process thought the freedom of each actual occasion makes it a "reason unto itself" (cf. Whitehead 1978, 45). Indeed, Whitehead suggests that creative synthesis is fundamentally regulated by the spontaneous self-creation of each momentary occasion:

> This process of the synthesis of subjective forms derived conformally is not settled by the antecedent fact of the data, for these data in their own separate natures do not carry any regulative principles for their synthesis. The regulative principle is derived from the novel unity which is imposed on them by the novel creature and process of constitution. Thus the immediate occasion from the spontaneity of its own essence must supply the missing determination for the synthesis of subjective form. (Whitehead 1933, 255)[6]

The antecedent data given to each occasion includes the occasions which make up the concrescing occasion's past, the aims and valuations of these past occasions, and the initial aim provided by the Primordial Nature of God (Whitehead 1933, 253 ff.). Although these data are necessary in the formation of the actual occasion, they do not determine the occasion's final synthesis. In other words, although the order and valuations of the given past and God's lure for feeling are given data in the process of an actual occasion's concrescence or self-creation, the concrescing occasion is ultimately autonomous in how it will synthesize these data. On the surface, therefore, it appears that creative synthesis rests upon spontaneous self-creation, which, by definition is arbitrary and has no norm outside itself. Thus, the one norm that might possibly be derived from spontaneous self-creation is that of "adventure" (cf. Whitehead 1933, 258). However, to take adventure as a norm amounts to a constant surpassing of the limits laid down by past actualizations and hence the continual destruction of the old order. Hence, adventure as the "ongoing perfectibility without determinant ends or limits leaves us with no criteria for the evaluation of the new perfection except the depth or intensity of the new experience, whatever it is" (Clark 1981, 137). (I will postpone discussion of the additional possibility of grounding justice and rights in intensity of experience or aesthetic satisfaction for the next subsection.)

I believe that these criticisms of novelty and autonomy rest upon assumptions which are not shared by process thinkers, in general, and certainly not by Cobb, in particular. The criticism that process thought takes newness or change as good, assumes that creative synthesis is equivalent to change in general. If creative synthesis is merely another term for change, critics would be correct in concluding that creative synthesis advocates change for its own sake, and thus is ultimately destructive of all order since change can be for the better or the worse. However, for Whitehead, there is a distinction between change which aims at the dissolution of order and change which aims at the creation of higher order.[7] The previous chapter has shown that Cobb makes a similar distinction between entropy and creative transformation. Creative transformation refers to Life, the creative process which makes possible attainment of progressive complexity and width in harmony of feeling. This sort of change "runs counter to the vast movements of change in the universe. Change in general in the physical world is described as entropy"—a movement from order to disorder (Birch & Cobb 1981, 184 f.). It is true that "in the temporal world, it is the empirical fact that [creative advance] entails loss [of previous forms of order]" (1978, 340); but the loss is loss of *lower* forms of order so as to make possible new, higher forms of order. That is, creative advance does not *aim* at dissolution of order, but at the attainment of higher forms of order. Although "Decay, Transition, Loss, Displacement belong to the essence of Creative advance" (Whitehead 1933, 286), they do so to the extent that they erode a given order that has grown stale, stifling, or oppressive, thus providing the opportunities for creative synthesis of new, higher forms of order. Hence, creative transformation points to a particular sort of change which aims at a particular sort of order, namely, at a "society permissive of actualities with patterned intensity of feeling arising from adjusted contrasts" (Whitehead 1978, 244). In short, creative advance refers to progress, the art of which "is to preserve order amid change, and to preserve change amid order" (1978, 339).

Second, the criticism that the spontaneity of creative synthesis abrogates the possibility of a norm governing actualization, assumes, first, that creative synthesis can be reduced to spontaneity, and, second, that spontaneity is mere arbitrariness. Admittedly, as quoted above, Whitehead asserts that the creative synthesis of an occasion of experience is determined autonomously, by "the spontaneity of its own essence" (1933, 255). In that quote, Whitehead also notes that spontaneity "must supply the *missing* determination" (italics added). That is, spontaneity is not the sole determinant of creative synthesis: there are the determinations provided by conformal feelings, that is, feelings conforming to the aims and valuations of past occasions and God. In other words, the determinants of the creative synthesis of a novel occasion are not reducible to spontaneity alone, but also include the occasion's prehension of past aims and the valuation of the Primordial Nature of God which is presented as a "graded relevance" of eternal objects (cf. Whitehead 1978, 244). God's graded envisagement of eternal objects refers to the possibilities for realization available to the actual occasion. These possibilities are both relevant to the occasion's given past, and graded or ordered in such a way that the occasion prehends an ideal possibility for realization along with other possibilities. Together, the past aims and God's graded envisagement of relevant eternal objects constitute the initial aim—to which Cobb adds God's consequent nature, that is, God's own feeling of the world (cf. Cobb 1965a, 156). As noted in chapter two, the prehension of this ideal aim is accompanied by a feeling of obligation, and is viewed by Cobb as the source of the feeling of moral obligation, that is, of right action (cf. Cobb 1965a, 96, 157). Hence, in attempting to reduce creative synthesis to spontaneity, critics fails to recognize one possible account of moral obligation that may answer the search for a principle of right order in process thought.

Moreover, a careful examination of the relationship of spontaneity to the initial aim in creative synthesis discloses that the spontaneity of an actual occasion is not mere arbitrariness. Spontaneity refers to the occasion's freedom to choose how it will actualize itself *within the limits of the graded envisagement of possibilities relative to the given past.* Freedom is hardly undirected self-assertion; rather, it is the capacity to transcend the givenness of the past within the limits provided by the initial aim. When Whitehead says that an occasion's initial data do not provide a regulative principle, he is not saying that they do not provide an *ideal* aim, nor that there are no limits to autonomy. Indeed, he is saying that the initial aim presents the occasion with possibilities which allow for and make possible autonomy. For without graded relevance of possibilities, there would be no grounds for spontaneity and free choice for there would be nothing upon which to exercise choice. Whitehead states clearly that,

> there is no such fact as absolute freedom; every actual
> entity possesses only such freedom as is inherent in
> the primary phase 'given' by its standpoint of rela-
> tivity to its actual universe.   Freedom, givenness,
> potentiality, are notions which presuppose each other
> and limit each other. (Whitehead 1978, 133)

Moreover, as we shall see in the next chapter, Cobb argues that freedom for future occasions is increased to the extent that the present occasion actualizes the initial ideal aim. Put differently, the capacity for human freedom is enhanced insofar as a person conforms to the initial ideal aim.

CRITIQUE OF AESTHETIC SATISFACTION

Aesthetic satisfaction—what Cobb generally calls "richness of experience," and Whitehead, "beauty"—is unequivocally a normative category for process thought and therefore is a likely candidate for grounding justice and rights by providing directionality for creative synthesis and interrelatedness. However, critics argue that to appeal to aesthetic satisfaction as a norm for justice and rights subordinates ethics to aesthetics. This criticism is most easily leveled at Hartshorne who states that "since the intrinsic value of experience is by definition aesthetic value, and since goodness is the disinterested will to enhance the value of future experiences, ethics presupposes aesthetics" (Hartshorne 1970, 308). Hartshorne's statement seems to be echoed in Cobb's statement that the "sense of obligation is brought by full disinterested consideration of all relevant factors to support that action which will increase intrinsic value. We will assume here the understanding of intrinsic value as strength of beauty" (Cobb 1965a, 122). The apparent implication is that just as it "is more important that a proposition be interesting [i.e., have beauty] than be true" (Whitehead 1978, 259), it is more important that an action or state of affairs be beautiful than be just.

Moreover, as as an ideal, aesthetic satisfaction refers to increasing intensification of experience, whereas justice "points to a limit beyond which no one can properly go in the pursuit of intensification of personal experience" (Clark 1981, 138). Whitehead suggests that there

> can be intense experience without harmony. In this event there is Destruction of the significant characters of individual objects. ... Discord consists in ... destruction. ... But even this discord may be preferable to a feeling of slow relapse into general anesthesia or into tameness which is its prelude. (Whitehead 1933, 263 f.)

Yet, it is possible to speak of the intensity of experience found in the challenge and excitement of a carefully executed murder. A good assassin might experience a great deal of aesthetic satisfaction in a complex and venturesome murder of an elusive target, and it seems possible that a disinterested observer could appreciate the aesthetic achievement, the complexity and intensity, of the assassin's action— which accounts in part for the lure of murder mysteries. But, on the basis of that aesthetic satisfaction alone, one would be hard-pressed to argue that the assassin's action was right.

First, in response to the question of subordinating ethics to aesthetics, it is beyond the limits of this essay to analyze Hartshorne's position with the care it deserves. It suffices, however, to note that Cobb is far from subordinating ethics to aesthetics. Rather, Cobb is suggesting that the sense of obligation—derived from the initial ideal aim and formulated as "One ought to do that which appears right on disinterested consideration of all relevant factors"—attaches to the principle that one ought to do that which will increase intrinsic value (cf. 1965a, 122). That is, for Cobb, the goal of attaining intrinsic value is not the ground of ethical obligation, it is commended by ethical obligation. Cobb's theory of value is not the basis for his theory of obligation; but this is not to say that obedience to one's obligation does not lead to beauty. In fact, if moral obligation is the feeling of obligation which accompanies the ideal aim given by God, then conformity to obligation leads to the greatest possible achievement of beauty possible for oneself and others affected by one's act. This point has been elucidated in detail above in chapter two.

Second, it would be an oversimplification to identify beauty entirely with intensity of experience. Although intensity of experience is necessary to aesthetic satisfaction, it is not a sufficient condition for attainment of beauty. Even the quote from Whitehead—that discord, as a result of intensity, "may be preferable"—cannot be construed as supporting the priority of intensity over harmony and width of experience, because the point of Whitehead's statement is that such discord is preferable insofar as it leads to a new aesthetic satisfaction which includes a wider harmony of intensity. To abstract intensity from harmony and width of experience is to fall into the fallacy of misplaced concreteness.

Although one might discern some aesthetic achievement in the complexity and intensity of the assassin's action—as we might admire the genius of a fictional murderer in a mystery novel—I do not think that the nature of aesthetic satisfaction would approve such an action as preferable under normal circumstances. Normally, in an assassination, the aesthetic satisfaction is extremely deficient insofar as it ignores the aim at value of the target and those whose aim at value is intimately bound up with the target, for example the target's family. Put differently, the assassin ignores her/his interrelatedness to others, and does not aim at a "wider harmony" of competing aims, which is an irreducible dimension of aesthetic satisfaction. However, it may be argued that the aesthetic achievement of assassinating a Hitler is morally preferable insofar as it removes a major obstacle to richness of experience for a wider constituency. Hence, Bonhoeffer's assassination plot can be recognized as morally necessary, and even heroic. Nevertheless, process thought would also see this sort of assassination as tragic inasmuch as it falls short of the ideal of creatively transforming even the likes of Hitler. Perhaps what many critics find objectionable is process thought's contention that the extreme discord resulting from the assassin's act can, at times, be taken up into subsequent harmonies or achievements of beauty. Of course, process thought does not assume that all discord is transformed into better harmonies—as Cobb points out, we may quite possibly destroy all life on this planet which will leave an immense loss, even in the aesthetic achievement of God. However, Cobb, like other theologians dealing with the problem of theodicy, believes that through creative transformation tragedies and suffering sometimes become vehicles for good—a theme which is certainly central to the story of the crucifixion of Jesus Christ.

Finally, it should be reiterated that for Cobb, aesthetic satisfaction is not the ground of moral obligation; rather, moral obligation is rooted in the subjective form of the prehension of the lure of creative synthesis embodied in the initial ideal aim. However, aesthetic satisfaction is related to creative synthesis, for insofar as aesthetic satisfaction refers to the achievement of intrinsic value in each individual, and insofar as each individual aims at some achievement of value, creative synthesis as the harmonizing of competing aims and influences, seeks the optimal achievement of value in oneself as well as others. Aesthetic satisfaction is both taken account of and the outcome of creative synthesis. However, because creative synthesis is relevant to and limited by a given situation, the maximum beauty attainable in that situation may be, and often is, tragic—such is the case with the assassination of a tyrant. Nonetheless, consideration of how one's actions affect the possible achievement of value in others does help one become more attentive to the lure of creative transformation. In short, the possible achievement of beauty for oneself and others is a relevant factor in one's moral obligation to conform to the initial ideal aim. Hence, in terms of Christian ethics, conformity to Christ as the central norm of Christian ethics also includes consideration of the interests of others. This observation leads to Cobb's understanding of rights and justice.

A PROCESS PERSPECTIVE OF JUSTICE

The criticisms of the ability of process thought to provide a grounding for justice and rights can be summarized in the contention that none of the categories of interrelatedness, creative synthesis, or aesthetic satisfaction is able to account for the essential elements of justice of the irreplaceable worth and dignity of determinate individuals which undergirds inviolability and equity. Moreover, as Stackhouse and other social ethicists argue, justice must contain a context invariant ideal, such as a normative view of human nature or a just procedure, which provides critical transcendence for evaluating the status quo, that is, for determining whether present and proposed institutions and practices are just. If these elements of justice are taken as necessary in some form, it would follow that Cobb's theory justice must account for individual dignity and equity, and provide a context invariant ideal.

The previous section showed that the common sense criticisms of the process categories of interrelatedness, creative synthesis, and beauty, are based upon incomplete or mistaken interpretations of these categories. It is also worth noting that those criticisms tend to overlook the interconnectedness of these categories in process thought. Although these categories are somewhat independent on an abstract level, they interpenetrate on the concrete level of existence. For example, an individual's attainment of richness of experience is dependent upon the individual's openness to creative synthesis and is enriched by interrelations with others. This section examines how Cobb draws upon these same categories to formulate the basis of a theory rights and justice that accounts for individual worth and personal equity, and points to what can be called a context invariant ideal. It will become clear that for Cobb each of these categories leads to consideration of the others. In general, I argue that Cobb grounds rights primarily in the capacity for aesthetic achievement, and equity primarily in interrelatedness, and finally, I argue that creative transformation provides a sort of context invariant ideal providing critical transcendence for socio-cultural criticism and change.

AESTHETIC SATISFACTION AS THE BASIS FOR RIGHTS

I have pointed out above that aesthetic satisfaction refers not only to the intensity, but also to the complexity and harmony of an experience. Cobb believes these elements taken together provide a criterion of comparative evaluation for determining beauty or richness of experience. Although Cobb's criterion is complex and perhaps, at times, difficult to apply, clearly, it is more directive than mere intensity of experience, and thus better suited to provide a normative guide to the moral obligation to increase value.

Cobb draws upon the category of aesthetic satisfaction to lay a possible groundwork for a theory of rights. As noted in chapter two, the locus of aesthetic satisfaction is the subjective immediacy of each individual occasion, so that each individual is a locus of intrinsic value. Even though its overall experience of value may be positive or negative, depending on its attainment of beauty or discord, each individual "achieves some measure of harmony out of the data provided it for its synthesis. In this sense, every occasion has some positive value" (1965a, 102). Since the "presence of beauty constitutes an occasion of experience as valuable, quite apart from its relation to any future beyond itself," each individual is valuable in itself (1965a, 104). Insofar as a nexus of occasions is the sum of its constituent occasions, it has intrinsic value—more so, insofar as the nexus is a living person, an ordered nexus coordinated by a serial order of dominant occasions which is "a single center of experience playing a decisive role in the functioning of the organism as a whole" (1965a, 48). Cobb notes that to acknowledge that an entity, (whether individual occasion or complex person), is intrinsically valuable is to acknowledge that it is an end in itself, as well as a means to the achievement of value of future entities (see Birch & Cobb 1981, 151). Moreover, the value of each entity is "irreplaceable" insofar as the entity, or its constituent occasions, constitutes a unique and unrepeatable concrescence of experience. Hence, Cobb derives a Kantian style principle from the recognition that all individuals are ends, as well as means, namely, that

> we should respect every entity for its intrinsic value as well as for its instrumental value to others, including ourselves. Its intrinsic value is the richness of its experience or of the experiences of its constituent parts. (Birch & Cobb 1981, 152)

Put differently, to recognize others as being ends in themselves is to recognize that they have inviolable worth and dignity. Cobb agrees with traditional social ethicists that the inviolable dignity and worth of the individual as an end in itself is the basis for affirming the rights of individuals (cf. Birch & Cobb 1981, 154). However, unlike many traditional social ethicists, Cobb does not take the notion of inviolability as pertaining to human beings only.

Although I find an intuitive appeal in Cobb's account of individual dignity, I think it is unfortunate that Cobb does not actually explain why recognition that others are ends in themselves implies that they ought to be respected. In other words, Cobb does not elucidate the relationship between the value of an entity for itself and the claim of that value on others. In part, Cobb appears to be appealing to empathy when he states that "if we, as subjects, are of value, and we are, there is every reason to think that other subjects are of value too. If our value is not only our usefulness to others but also our immediate enjoyment of our existence, this is true for other creatures as well" (Birch & Cobb 1981, 151). Hence, through empathy we not only realize that our claim for respect for our own worth is shared by others, we also experience their claim on us. If this is taken as the central basis for respect of others' dignity, then, it appears that respect for individual inviolability is a requirement of love. On this point, Cobb's position does not appear too far from Reinhold Niebuhr who, like many other traditional Christian social ethicists, makes a very strong case that love both demands justice as a minimum while also transcending it (cf. Niebuhr 1943, 244-247).[8] Additionally, the duty to respect others as ends in themselves might have some basis in the general duty, mentioned above, that we ought to enhance intrinsic value. Insofar as we are morally bound to increase richness of experience in others as well as ourselves, we are bound to enhance the possibilities for others to achieve intrinsic value. At minimum, this would seem to include that we ought to respect others as ends.

That all creatures should be respected as ends as well as means implies that all creatures have claims upon others, and hence that all creatures have certain rights. This means that the subhuman world also has rights, for even animals experience intrinsic value and so must be considered as ends, and not means only. Thus, Cobb notes that "Kant's doctrine of the Kingdom of Ends must be vastly expanded" (Birch & Cobb 1981, 151). For critics, this difference may seem to extend inviolability so far that it loses any significance for human rights. In response to this sort of criticism, Cobb is quick to point out that

> theoretical commitment to a model which treats all human beings as having intrinsic value while regarding everything else as valuable only in the service of human beings does not [de facto] protect most human beings [women, minorities, etc.] from being valued only for their use to the dominant classes. (Birch & Cobb 1981, 283)

Hence, what is needed is a model that accounts for the respective rights of all creatures since all creatures have intrinsic worth.

Notwithstanding the failure of anthropocentric models of justice, the extension of rights to subhumanity raises a problem, namely, do all creatures have equal rights, so that the right of a chicken to life is comparable to the right of a human being to life? Cobb suggests that the rights of entities correlates to their capacities for experiencing intrinsic value. That is, the rights of entities are in proportion to their capacities for richness of experience or aesthetic satisfaction.

Cobb's description of some of the levels of capacities for richness of experience admittedly offers only general guidelines: inorganic entities have less capacity than do living cells; plants have less capacity than do animals; animals with little or no nervous system have less capacity than animals, such as humans, which have highly developed nervous systems (Birch & Cobb 1981, 152 f.). Cobb acknowledges that richness of experience offers a somewhat "crude" criterion for distinguishing among the rights of subhuman entities, but holds that it still offers "considerable practical guidance" (Birch & Cobb 1981, 154). Rocks and plants have little capacity for richness of experience, and so, for the most part, can be treated instrumentally; whereas highly developed animals such as porpoises, chimpanzees, and, of course human beings, have much greater capacity for richness of experience, and so their claims upon others is greater. Hence, in general, Cobb believes that the criterion of capacity for richness of experience offers justification for such guidelines as the United States Humane Society's principles for the treatment of animals, for example, that "it is wrong to kill animals needlessly or for entertainment or to cause animals pain or torment" (Birch & Cobb 1981, 155).

However, it should be noted that Cobb believes that consideration of the claims of the subhuman world needs to be extended beyond concern for the rights of individual animals. For example, the Humane Society's concern for individual animals tends to focus upon the rights of animals directly under the care of human beings, but it does not address the destruction of wilderness habitats which threatens the survival of entire species of animals, not to mention plants (Birch & Cobb 1981, 169). At this point, Cobb introduces the notion of "species rights" and the "rights of ecosystems" (Birch & Cobb 1981, 170). Indeed, Cobb goes so far as to state that "the right of the species to survival is much more fundamental than the right of the individual member to life" (Birch & Cobb 1981, 170). This statement could be interpreted to mean that individual rights are necessarily sacrificed when they conflict with the needs of the species. If this were the case, there would be little meaning to the notion of individual inviolability. But such an interpretation would fail to recognize that Cobb is not referring to the relationship between the rights of an individual and the rights of the species to which it belongs. Rather, he is comparing the strength of the claim of an individual animal upon humanity with the strength of the claim of an entire species upon humanity. The claim of an individual animal not to be killed by humanity, for example, for food, is not as great as the claim of a species not to be decimated in fulfilling food needs.

The basis of a species' rights appears, in part, to be the sum of the rights of the individuals which constitute it. For example, some individual animals, such as insects, may have little potential for rich experience, and thus, little individual claim upon human beings; but their species as a whole, has greater potential for rich experience, and hence, greater species rights. In part, Cobb also appears to appeal to the notion that the various species exist in an interdependent web of life, which, in some of his writings, Cobb pictures as a "biotic pyramid," "beginning with the soil and proceeding through insects, plants, birds, rodents, to the larger carnivores, and finally to man [and woman]" (1972b, 55).[9] This image of a pyramid not only illustrates the levels of potentiality for richness of experience, but also the mutual interrelatedness of the various levels. Just as the apex of a pyramid would be precarious without an adequately wide base, the stability of the biotic pyramid would degenerate without the diversity among the species at each level, and the potential for richness of experience at the higher levels would be impoverished without the existence of the lower levels. Hence, Cobb suggests that the individuals, species, and even ecosystems, which make up the biotic pyramid can be viewed as having claims upon humanity, not only in themselves, but also in terms of the value they have for one another and for the world.

> All things have a *right* to be treated the way they *ought* to be treated for their own sake. But it is not possible to decide how to deal with an individual animal, species or ecosystem apart from a general view of the sort of world envisaged as being worth bringing into being. At this point a sense of the web of life, the value of diversity, and the way people are constituted by internal relations to others, will all guide the imagination. (Birch & Cobb 1981, 170)

In other words, our recognition of the rights of species and ecosystems is, in a sense, augmented by our realization that species and ecosystems contribute to the value of a wider, interconnected environment. This observation points to a theological dimension of Cobb's view of rights, for implicit in Cobb's view is the conviction that the value of both individuals and of their environmental interrelationships are ultimately enjoyed by God, for whom all individuals, species, and ecosystems have everlasting significance. Hence, Cobb affirms

> that from the point of view of process theologians, justice requires that the rest of the creation should also be treated with respect and recognised to have reality and value quite apart from usefulness to human beings. Other creatures are of value in themselves and for God. (1982b, 132)

It should be noted that Cobb's observations on the rights of the subhuman world illustrate his presupposition of the concrete interrelationship of the categories under consideration. I will return to the further significance of interrelatedness for rights and justice in the following subsection.

To illustrate how the capacity for richness of experience can serve as a measure of rights due individuals at different levels of the biotic pyramid, Cobb compares the right to life of a human being with the right to life of a chicken. A chicken and a human being are both ends in themselves, and hence place claims upon others. However, we generally assume that it is permissible to kill a chicken for the benefit of a human being, say, for food; but we do not generally think it is permissible to kill one human being for the benefit of another. Cobb notes three factors ingredient in a human being's capacity for rich experience that are relevant to the right to life (i.e., not to be killed): (a) a human being has future potential for unique and ever greater intrinsic value which is irretrievably lost when she is deprived of life; (b) a human being is self-conscious thus aware that she will die, and "fear that one's life will be cut off in mid-stream" brings more suffering/anxiety (i.e., possible loss of the capacity for rich experience) than fear of death at the end of a full life; and (c) the interrelatedness of a human being to other human beings is such that the "death of one person has consequences for others" in the community—pain, loss, grief—that bring suffering (Birch & Cobb 1981, 158 f.). The capacity for rich experience in a chicken is hardly comparable, and thus does not warrant as strong a claim to life: (a) a chicken's future potential for unique and greater intrinsic value is so trivial that if its death "makes room for raising another" chicken, there is little loss in value; (b) a chicken is not self-consciousness, and thus is not affected by anticipation of death so long as it is not killed in ways that increase its immediate terror and suffering; and (c) the interrelatedness of a chicken to its society is such that its death does not appear to induce experience of grief or loss (Birch & Cobb 1981, 159).

What is noteworthy in the comparison of the basis of the right to life of a human being with that of a chicken is certainly not that it is often permissible to kill a chicken, for example, for food; rather it is that the chicken's right to life is not without some significance. A chicken's capacity for some richness of experience indicates that taking its life is not a casual matter, but requires some justification and is subject to limitations. For example, Cobb implies that the loss of value resulting from the death of a chicken is in part justified if it makes room for the raising of another, hence ensuring the survival of the species; and the killing of a chicken, when justified, should not be cruel and prolonged, but as painless and quick as possible. What applies to the consideration of a chicken's right to life applies all the more to higher animals. Indeed, when considering the right to life of chimpanzees or porpoises, we must recognize that these animals possesses a high degree of individuality, self-consciousness, and capacity for grief, to such an extent that "the considerations that lead to opposing the killing of human beings count also against the killing of some animals" (Birch & Cobb 1981, 160). Hence, for Cobb, such practices as animal experimentation on chimpanzees and the killing of porpoises in tuna fishing are, for the most part, a violation of these animals' right to life, for pretty much the same reasons as human experimentation and the killing of persons as means to produce food are violations of human rights (cf. Birch & Cobb 1981, 160 f.).

Although the capacity for richness of experience is helpful in determining the relative rights among species, it is less helpful in determining the relative rights of members within a species. Indeed, Cobb notes that it can generally be assumed that members of the same species have roughly equal capacities for richness of experience, and thus, there is little practical reason for examining relative value, hence rights, of some members in comparison with others (Birch & Cobb 1981, 163). Nonetheless, Cobb recognizes that the question of relative value and rights is important within the human species. There are differences among human individuals' capacities for rich experience; differences that may be due to culture, or genetic inheritance, or proximity to the "fringes" of life and death. How do individuals' differences affect their claims on others? This question raises the problem of equity.

RELATEDNESS AS A BASIS FOR EQUITY

Before turning to the issue of equity, it is interesting to note how different Cobb's understanding of the moral implications of interrelatedness or internal relations is from Stackhouse's and Clark's.

Stackhouse and Clark believe that the emphasis upon internal relatedness contradicts respect for individual dignity because it minimizes recognition of the separateness and independence of others which, for them, is fundamental to both traditional and modern views of justice. Hence, they believe that emphasis upon interrelatedness tends to obscure the boundaries between individuals that ensure against manipulation and use of others for one's own advantage (cf. Clark 1981, 136). Cobb's understanding of rights indicates that he would agree that individual inviolability, even if not absolute, is fundamental to justice. However, as noted in the previous subsection, for Cobb, it is by virtue of the interrelatedness of individuals, which makes empathy possible, that individuals recognize that others ought to be treated as ends in themselves. Indeed, Cobb's approach to interrelatedness turns Stackhouse's and Clark's criticisms around by suggesting that over-emphasis upon separateness, upon external relatedness, leads to objectifying others and to a failure to appreciate others' subjectivity and thus their value to themselves. Cobb notes that this has even been true of our attitude toward the society of living cells which make up our own body. The Cartesian dualism which conceives of our bodies as fundamentally separated from ourselves has supported the view of "our bodies as objects to be used and controlled rather than as fully continuous with ourselves" (Birch & Cobb 1981, 187). If we objectify our own bodies and see them as objects for manipulation, how much more do we objectify others and view them as means to our private desires and ends? To view others as externally related to us encourages objectification of others, seeing them as means only, hence, as things to be manipulated and used for achieving our own interests. To recognize our internal relatedness to others "can break us out of this objectifying attitude. We are parts of one society in which each has a role to play for the sake of the others" (Birch & Cobb 1981, 187).

Granted that awareness of interrelatedness helps us to recognize others as ends in themselves and to break down manipulative and objectifying attitudes and behavior, there are, nevertheless, such dramatic differences among human beings that it might seem justifiable to treat those who have little capacity for rich experience more as means than as ends in themselves—just as it is justifiable to treat certain subhumans more as means than as ends. Put in the form of a question: If rights are correlative with the capacity or potential for richness of experience, can Cobb account for the kind of personal equity that advocates of social justice call for? This problem is precisely what a theory of justice must illuminate. For example, what is the basis of the rights of a seriously handicapped child, say, with Down's syndrome, whose capacity for rich experience is seriously limited? Or what is the basis of the rights of persons whose cultures have denied them the opportunity to develop their capacity and potential for rich experience? Or what right does an unborn fetus have to life, or a terminally ill patient who wants to die? Does an incapacity for potential rich experience mean that these persons may or should be treated less as ends in themselves than so-called normal persons?[10]

First, it must be noted that unlike most other species of animals, "where the unified animal experience primarily functions in the service of the body, in human beings it aims at its own richness of experience and frequently subordinates the body to these aims" (Birch & Cobb 1981, 162). This fact, together with the fact that human beings are self-conscious, and thus capable of much more complex and intense levels of experience than most other species, means that "human beings are *primarily* ends and only secondarily means" (Birch & Cobb 1981, 162, italics added). It is misleading to think that the capacity for rich experience in human beings with severe limitations, even in a child with Down's syndrome, is at such a level that we could consider such individuals as primarily means rather than as ends, for in most cases the aim at rich experience still subordinates the aims of the body, and there remains a significant level of self-consciousness. Nonetheless, given that the capacity for rich experience in severely limited persons is still measurably less than in those without those limitations, are the rights of those limited individuals less than those without limitations? Put differently, if "there is no substantial reason to believe that all persons have equal intrinsic value ... [d]oes it open the gates to all sorts of inhumanity" (Birch & Cobb 1981, 164)?

Of course, Cobb emphatically answers "No." Cobb takes the recognition that there are unequal attainments in richness of experience to be enough reason to recognize the principle that we "ought to promote richness of experience wherever possible" (Birch & Cobb 1981, 164). Hence, we ought to do what we can to help those with limitations overcome those limitations so that they can attain an increased capacity for richness of experience. This principle, as noted above, derives from the fundamental experience of obligation. Here, however, Cobb also links it to our interrelatedness with one another by drawing upon John Rawls' insight that because "we share one another's fate," we, as a community, become "responsible for the deprived through every responsible member of that community" (Birch & Cobb 1981, 165; cf. Rawls 1971, 102).

That this is an implicit appeal to an empathetic consideration of others with limited capacities for rich experience is illustrated by Cobb's consideration of our responsibility to those with genetic handicaps:

> If I am more or less normal, it is through no merit of my own. That others have enormous burdens to bear may be no fault of theirs. The child with Down's syndrome could have been me. The fact that others are lacking, through no fault of theirs, changes for me the character of my having. If there is any meaning to the unity of humankind then all are called to share the cost. (Birch & Cobb 1981, 164 f.)

By reason of an empathetic appreciation of our interrelatedness, we are called to share in both the goods and burdens of others. What we owe to others, therefore, is determined not merely by their capacity for richness of experience, but also by our interrelatedness and sharing of a common fate. This, for Cobb, is the basis of equity.[11]

What has been said of the special claims of those who suffer from physical and mental limitations holds true in a similar manner for those who have been limited by cultural practices, such as sexism, racism, and classism, which deny some groups and individuals opportunities to flourish. Cobb notes that such practices have often led to severe limitations in persons' capacity for rich experience, resulting in "an actual inferiority of experiences on the part of slaves, peasants, women, ethnic minorities and other classes," which "has been appealed to as justifying the practices which created it" (Birch & Cobb 1981, 165). To recognize that these persons are interrelated with us is to recognize that we not only share one another's fate, but that we share in the practices that have led to their incapacities. Hence, equity requires that we "reverse [these] prac-

tice[s] by providing equal, and in some cases compensatory, opportunities for those sub-cultures to which these opportunities have for
so long been denied" (Birch & Cobb 1981, 165).

In general, Cobb understands equity to entail equality of opportunity for all to develop their capacity for rich experience. When
that opportunity is deficient due to circumstances beyond the individual's control, for example, because of accident of birth or cultural
denial, then all are called to help alleviate or counter those deficiencies. Cobb observes that this view "does not differ substantially
from conclusions often reached on the basis of the absolutist view"
that all human beings have infinite, inviolable worth (Birch & Cobb
1981, 166). However, because Cobb does not have an absolutist
view of rights, he differs on issues "at the fringes" of life at death.
This difference is illustrated in his view of abortion.

Cobb rejects the view that any human being, and a fortiori
any fetus, has absolute worth at any one stage of development. On
the other hand, he does affirm that even the "fertilised egg already has
some intrinsic value," and, therefore, the fetus has some rights:
"increasing rights as time passes, but these rights are less than those
of the newly born infant, and they must always be considered in
connection with the rights of others" (Birch & Cobb 1981, 166 f.).
Hence, Cobb neither accepts the absolute right of the mother over the
fetus nor the absolute right of the fetus to life:

> The notions that the mother should have the absolute
> right to decide about the contents of her womb, or
> that the foetus is no more than an unneeded ap-
> pendage of her body, are not justified by this ac-
> count. On the other hand, the foetus does not have
> the same rights as a fully developed human being.
> (Birch & Cobb 1981, 167)

Moreover, the question of abortion cannot be limited to the
relative rights of mother and fetus. Because both mother and fetus are
interdependent members of other societies—of family, community,
and an overcrowded world—one must also consider the rights of the
father, other children, other relatives, and the larger society (Birch &
Cobb 1981, 167). Of course, unwanted children are best avoided by
avoiding pregnancy, but there are cases "where it is too late for

avoidance," and consideration of the relevant rights may lead to a decision to abort. Elsewhere, Cobb has suggested that in a growing number of situations, especially in the two-thirds world where birth control techniques and education are extremely expensive and difficult to make available, larger societal concern for limiting population has become a rightful factor in permitting abortion (see 1972b, 67-73). At the same time Cobb affirms that even such "global considerations do not overrule the rights of the foetus and the relatives" (Birch & Cobb 1981, 167), because society as a whole, or the state, has instrumental value only (1972b, 70). Hence, it is not only important that those making the decision about abortion should consider the needs and resources of society, it is important that society support the mother and relatives in their decision, whether that is for abortion or for birth.

Cobb's observation about the relationship of society, especially political society, to individuals points to an important aspect of his understanding of relatedness. As noted above, common observation indicates that the unity and identity that we associate with selfhood appears most clearly in those creatures who have the greatest capacity for interrelatedness. This observation tends to confirm Cobb's view that persons are dipolar; that is, persons are neither mere bundles of relations nor self-contained individuals. Morally, however, Cobb places emphasis upon the intrinsic value of persons, but notes that "the individuals who have [intrinsic] value are constituted by the society, as well as together constituting the society for each other" (Cobb 1981b, 19). Hence, Cobb's view of interrelatedness does not submerge the rights of the individual in concern for the organic whole, but does require that concern for the whole, especially the welfare of the planet, at least "become a factor in shaping public policy" (Birch & Cobb 1981, 167).

In short, Cobb affirms "liberal individualistic humanism" in the sense that he believes that "there is no society that is more than, or other than, the individuals who compose it" (1981b, 19). But, by the same token, he affirms that individuals are "social through and through" (1981b, 19). This view, Cobb notes, has an important implication for social change and hence, I might add, for implementing justice. Any program "to change the structure of the society is to change individuals and to change individuals is to change the social context constitutive for all" (1981b, 19). Hence, implementing justice involves both a proper relationship to other individuals and a proper ordering of the structures of society.

The difficulty in applying equity to concrete situations is illustrated by the problem of allocation of scarce resources, for example, scarce medical resources. This problem is probably most dramatic in deciding who is able to have access to expensive and esoteric forms of surgical and medical treatment such as vital organ transplants, and more recently, in experimental treatment of Acquired Immune Deficiency Syndrome (AIDS). When tragic choices must be made so that some will be offered and some denied a chance at possible life-saving treatment, Cobb turns to the criterion of richness of experience. Specifically, Cobb states

> There is no rational way of solving these problems except by measuring alternative proposals in terms of the contribution each makes to enriching human experience. ... In making such a choice we have to deliberate in assessing both the intrinsic value and instrumental value of individual persons. ... We will never be sure whether our judgments in these matters of life and death are correct, but since we must decide, we should bring to bear such wisdom as we can. (Birch & Cobb 1981, 210)

Hence, Cobb believes it is better to provide such treatment to a common laborer with a family of five and deny it to a professional person with no family, because, given that the two persons have equal intrinsic value, the choice must be made on the basis of their differential instrumental value.

Lest it appear that Cobb is ultimately relying on a modified utilitarian principle as a basis for equity, it should be pointed out that Cobb turns to instrumental value only as a means for adjudicating among otherwise equally valid claims. Cobb not only finds these dilemmas tragic, he also argues that we need to consider the underlying factors that have led to these dilemmas. Hence, Cobb argues that such dilemmas are ultimately resolved by changing the structures of society to allow for more just institutions and procedures to ensure individual rights and equity. This raises the question of what context invariant ideal Cobb is able to appeal to for guiding social criticism and recommending social change.

CREATIVE SYNTHESIS AS A BASIS FOR SOCIAL CRITICISM AND
SOCIAL CHANGE

Although Cobb's theory of rights and equity is still in need
of refinement and elaboration, for example, in clarifying the relationship of empathy to rights and equity, I think that Cobb offers a viable basis for an understanding of rights and equity that satisfies two
of the central criteria for a theory of justice. However, critics have
also pointed out that justice requires a context invariant ideal which
transcends the flux of events so as to provide a perspective of critical
transcendence. I agree that if there is no way to transcend the status
quo, there is no way to give guidance to social changes that will produce a more just society. At the same time, I think the notion of a
context invariant ideal is somewhat ambiguous. Critics, like
Stackhouse and Clark, argue that process thought is constitutionally
incapable of offering any context invariant notions since process
thought views all reality as changing. But the validity of this criticism depends upon what level of abstraction one is considering. God
is certainly context variant, because God always changes in relation
to God's prehension of the world. Yet God is context invariant in the
sense that God exists and aims at realization of maximal beauty no
matter what changes are taking place in the world—or even if the
world as we know it has ceased to exist. Similarly, the notion of
creative transformation is context variant insofar as it refers to the
perpetually renewing reality of Christ or to the most appropriate initial ideal aim for any given moment. However, as an abstraction,
creative transformation is context invariant insofar as it refers to a
particular type of change, namely, the aim at novel integration of
conflicting goals. Indeed, Cobb specifically appeals to creative
transformation as the norm for critiquing and guiding social change.
I suggest that, as an ideal kind of change, Cobb's understanding of
creative transformation can be understood as a context invariant ideal
which can offer critical transcendence and guidance for social transformation. The rest of this section examines creative transformation
as a critical ideal for social change and briefly looks at an additional
element of contemporary justice, besides rights and equity, that this
ideal calls for.

Cobb compares the nature of creative transformative change with other forms of social and political change in the essay, *The Political Implications of Whitehead's Philosophy* (1981b). A society (or individual) can appropriate the potentially conflicting or competing influences and aims given in the data of its past and the graded relevant possibilities provided by God in several ways. First, it can *defend* against change by attempting to preserve a particular portion of the past as much as possible, realizing only novel possibilities that are easily compatible with that past, and blocking out aims and possibilities which diverge from that past (1981b, 20). A society can change by simply *capitulating* to an alternative, competing influence, substituting one for the other. It can change by simply *adding* new influences to its present structures without attempting to contrast or integrate them, such as an individual adding "new information or ideas to an established stock" without comparing it with previous knowledge or arriving at deeper insight (1981b, 20). A society can change by *compromising* among competing influences, modifying each so as to arrive at a moderate position (1981b, 20). It can take a more radical approach to change by *dialectically* opposing an entrenched influence of a particular past with radically different influences and rejecting the entrenched past with the hope that "a new position may emerge that resolves [the] opposition [of entrenched past and alternative influences] in a higher synthesis" (1981b, 21).

However, Cobb believes that all of these types of change ultimately lead to some form of disorder or entropy. Defensive change leads to repetition, and repetition inevitably leads to dénouement and dissolution. Capitulation echoes critics' characterization of undirected change, which is nihilistic (cf. Clark 1981, 137). Addition without integration leads eventually to fragmentation. Compromise amounts to a weakening or gradual trivialization of both competing influences. Dialectical negation, though it may sometimes lead to a "creative and original synthesis" of both entrenched past and radically alternative influences, can just as easily lead to loss of the past, and thus amount to capitulation and nihilism.

Cobb suggests that alternative to these sorts of changes is creative synthesis or creative transformation, involving the appreciation of competing influences and aims in their full integrity (1981b, 21). Creative transformation points to "the conversion of mere diversity [of competing aims] into contrast through mental originality. It is the fundamental model of growth in distinction from mere change or even quantitative addition" (1981b, 21). This sort of change converts or transforms competing and contradictory aims into a "harmony of contrasts" or an ordered unity that allows for diversity. Moreover, as the previous chapter has shown, creative transformative change is also experienced as transcending human effort and imagination—it is the change made possible by the creative good, and hence is to be served and trusted.

Although this analysis of creative transformative change can be supplemented further by what has been said about Life and creative transformation in the previous chapter, there remains a vagueness to Cobb's analysis that is a bit disconcerting for those wanting neatly defined principles by which to assess social change. In part, this vagueness is due to Cobb's tendency to draw most of his concrete examples of creative transformation from the realm of personal experience rather than from political experience. For example, in the essay *The Political Implications of Whitehead's Philosophy*, Cobb's examples of creative transformation are drawn from the experience of learning rather than from political change. This is unfortunate, because there are significant examples of creative transformation in the political arena that Cobb could draw upon. Perhaps the most obvious are the movements of Mohatma Gandhi and Martin Luther King, Jr. (and more recently, one could add the non-violent *coup* in the Philippines). Although these are not perfect embodiments of creative transformation, they point to changes which have attempted to integrate or reconcile largely opposing aims into a novel vision for changing their respective societies. These examples, at least indicate ways that creative transformation has been a significant factor in socio-political change.

However, there remains an inevitable vagueness to the analysis of creative transformation because at the heart of creative transformation is novelty, which by definition, cannot be prescribed beforehand. The sort of creative transformation that has occurred in the past is not identical to present opportunities for creative transformation because the present requires new visions and new possibilities which have not been realized before. Nonetheless, recognition of actual occurrences of creative transformation does make us aware of how we can be more sensitive and open to novel possibilities for change, and it provides some basis for hope that such change is possible in the future. Hence, even though examples of creative transformation do not provide us with neatly defined principles for designing social change, they do point to the sorts of attitudes and characteristics which have made creative transformation possible.

It may also be asked whether creative transformation is ultimately flawed because it would lead to acknowledgment of forces and ideologies in society which are so evil that they ought not be integrated in any form of social change: Could a movement like Nazism ever be recognized in its integrity so as to be taken up into a new creative vision of society (cf. Hartshorne 1970, 240)? Cobb, of course, acknowledges that "there are movements such as Nazism and the Ku Klux Klan in which Christians do not recognize the requisite . . . integrity" to allow them to be positive elements in social transformation. Although Cobb does not explain why rejection of such movements does not contradict the ideal of creative transformation, it is not hard to comprehend why this is the case. Movements such as Nazism and other organized ideologies of racism, sexism, and classism, seek not only to exclude diverse influences, but also to destroy them. Thus, these movements are fundamentally opposed to creative transformation, and therefore cannot be recognized as having integrity in any attempt to transform society creatively. However, this does not mean that individuals who are members of the Nazis or the Ku Klux Klan cannot be creatively transformed; but, they would no longer be Nazis or Klansmen. By way of theological analogy, to say that God is supremely loving does not mean that God loves evil, but it is to say that God nonetheless loves people who do evil. God's love does not make evil good, but it can make evil persons into good persons. This is the nature of conversion, which, for Cobb, is an archetypal example of creative transformation.

Does creative transformative change necessarily indicate change toward a more just society? Insofar as justice refers to an ordering of relationships that apportions to each what is her or his due so that each can mutually pursue her or his interests, it would seem that a process understanding of creative transformation implies, at the least, a consideration of justice, and, at the most, points to a notion of "right order." Just as justice refers to the ideal coincidence of the interests of all individuals with each other, thus with society as a whole; so too, creative transformation aims at harmonizing competing aims and influences, so as to achieve the optimal achievement of value for both others and oneself. At this formal level, I see little difference between the ideal of justice and the ideal of the creative transformation, unless it is taken a priori that the ideal of justice refers to a fixed utopia. Since a long tradition of Christian social ethics, including Stackhouse and Clark, does not understand justice in this sense, I assume that utopianism is not the only basis of a the context invariant ideal. Rather, I take it that the notion of justice is context invariant in the sense that it refers to an abstract ideal of mutually achievable interests. Justice is nonetheless context variant in the sense that it refers to what is possible to achieve in the given circumstances of a particular political and economic situation. Creative transformation is certainly context invariant and variant in the same ways as justice.

Moreover, the context variant dimension of creative transformation does not mean that strict principles of rights and equity are necessarily antithetical to creative transformative change, for such change can be encouraged by principles (cf. Birch & Cobb 1981, 144). I suggest that principles can be understood analogously to habit and discipline, which, as Cobb notes, "may either serve Life [creative transformation] or oppose it" (Birch & Cobb 1981, 185). However, any principles of rights and justice must themselves be open to creative transformation. Hence, strict adherence to principles is right insofar as those principles serve creative transformation.

I have noted that Cobb's understanding of rights and claims to equity take into consideration not just human rights and claims, but also the rights and claims of the subhuman world. Not surprisingly, in focussing on the issue of social transformation, Cobb is concerned with the global society, of which human political and economic life is but a part. However, Cobb's ecological sensitivity has made him aware of the competition between claims of human social rights and justice, on the one hand, and the claims of subhuman rights and justice, on the other. This competition can be understood as a fundamental case of allocation of scarce resources.

Progress in human justice and rights is usually associated with economic development through increased industrialization, urbanization, and agribusiness, which will provide an expanding horizon of opportunities to all persons. However, progress in ecological sustainability is associated with limits on industrialization, urbanization, and agribusiness, to allow nature to heal previously in-

flicted wounds of pollution, deforestation, and destruction of farm-
land. Cobb recognizes that "those who emphasise justice sometimes
see sustainability as the cry of those who benefit from present structures of society and want to distract attention from the abuses of
power within it" (Birch & Cobb 1981, 235). However, Cobb argues
that the creative transformation of the present structures of political
and economic life requires recognition that the goals of political justice and ecological sustainability ultimately serve each other. For
Cobb, this recognition is exemplified in the World Council of
Churches' declaration that Christians must work for a just, partici-
patory, and sustainable society (Birch & Cobb 1981, 235, 240).

Cobb notes that a truly just society is just to future generations, which means it must hand on a sustainable world, or future
generations will be denied opportunities commensurate with the present generation (Birch & Cobb 1981, 236). Moreover, present attempts to achieve world-wide justice are ultimately impossible unless
there is also a simultaneous attempt to ensure sustainability. For
example, to seek for a more just distribution of the world's wealth by
attempting to bring all countries up to the level of consumption in
the United States would be physically impossible and ecologically
disastrous (Birch & Cobb 1981, 246 f.). A more just distribution of
resources will have to be accompanied by programs which ensure
sustainability, including decreased consumption in first-world countries along with increased consumption in the two-thirds world.
Cobb adds that "the greatest threat to sustainability is war and the
preparations for war" which in 1980, before the Reagan adminis-
tration's massive military build-up, meant an expenditure of about
one million dollars per minute (Birch & Cobb 1981, 249). To make
a serious reduction in the arms race would not only reduce the pressure put on the environment by decreasing the use of non-renewable
resources such as metals and oil, it would also free funds, labor, and
resources to ameliorate world-wide health problems which hit hardest
in the two-thirds world (Birch & Cobb 1981, 249). In short, a vision
of a sustainable world implies a vision of a world where "there is
enough for everyone's need but not enough for everyone's greed"
(Birch & Cobb 1981, 251).

CONCLUSIONS

I have argued that Cobb's theory of justice fulfills the requirements put forth by critics concerned for social justice, namely, that justice provide an understanding of right order that safeguards personal inviolability and equity. However, for Cobb, there is no reason not to extend the meaning of justice to the subhuman world. Thus, Cobb is concerned with the rights and equitable treatment of animals, species, and ecosystems, as well as human rights and equity. By providing a basis for a theory of rights and justice which takes into account the ecological crisis as well as human political and economic concerns, Cobb is able to link the form and substance of his overall ecological ethic to the more conventional issues of social justice. Indeed, this is a transformed social ethic in which human political justice is given a broader and richer grounding by its concern for ecological sustainability.

Although Cobb does not devote much attention to the relationship between authentic Christian existence and rights and justice, it should be clear from what has been said thus far that conformation to Christ as creative transformation entails respect for others' rights and the pursuit of justice. Moreover, respect for rights and the pursuit of justice can serve to open one to the lure of creative transformation. To make explicit what Cobb leaves implicit, the justice that Cobb's theory points to can be called justice as creative transformation. The recognition that creative transformation is the core of Cobb's theory of justice indicates the persistence of a fundamental theological dimension in Cobb's ethics. Put in conventional theological language, for Cobb, justice has to do with implementing the Kingdom of Christ on earth—a dynamic kingdom that includes not just humanity, but all creation.

As I have pointed out above, Cobb's theory of justice still requires further refinement and elaboration. In particular, I believe that Cobb needs to work out more explicitly the relationship he sees between love and justice. I have suggested that underlying the relationship between the intrinsic value of individuals and the dignity or claim of individuals upon others for respect as ends in themselves is an implicit appeal to empathy—which is a central dimension of Cobb's view of love. Cobb makes a similar appeal to empathy in his discussion of equity as based upon sharing one another's fate.

Although Cobb makes no attempt that I know of to subordinate the principle of justice to love, it does seem that the elements of justice—personal inviolability and equity—can be interpreted as expressions of love as empathy. This interpretation, if correct, complements Niebuhr's view that love requires justice. Indeed, if justice can be understood as an expression of creative transformation, then it can be interpreted as an expression of Christian love.

Cobb's theory of justice offers, I believe, a viable alternative to traditional and modern theories of justice, such as natural law theory and the procedural justice of Rawls. Indeed, Cobb's theory seems to incorporate concerns found in both. Natural law theory is generally concerned that rights and justice conform with what we can know about reality, particularly, "the Good." However, it tends to conceive of reality as a static absolute, and limits the sphere of rights and justice to what is known of the human good. Cobb is interested in elucidating the implications of a process view of reality for rights and justice (cf. Birch & Cobb 1981, 141, 151). However, a process view of reality does not take itself or reality as absolute, and it does not arbitrarily limit the sphere of rights and justice to the human good. Rawls is concerned with providing procedures for determining what is just, without providing a metaphysical theory of the Good. However, Rawls also limits his consideration of justice to "moral personalities," which for him excludes the subhuman world. Cobb clearly finds Rawls' position amenable, as is illustrated by his appeal to Rawls' view of equity as involving sharing one another's fate and equality of opportunity (see Birch & Cobb 1981, 165, 236). However, Cobb does not divorce justice from metaphysical considerations of the Good, namely, richness of experience, and rejects the anthropocentric assumption, shared by traditional natural law theorists, that the subhuman world is not included in the domain of justice.

The question of whether Cobb's ecological concerns also support the concern for political and economic liberation remains. Hence, I turn to the question of whether process theology can support the aims of political and liberation theologies.

NOTES

1. Much of the analysis and argument in this chapter is indebted to Max Stackhouse's former student, Henry W. Clark, whose critique of process thought as a basis for a theory of justice and rights is presented in a cursory fashion in his published article, "Process Thought and Justice" (Clark 1981), and elaborated in considerable detail in his unpublished dissertation, *Dimensions of Justice and Process Thought* (Clark 1984), available through University Microfilms International, Ann Arbor, Michigan. The reasons for drawing upon Clark's work are twofold. First, to date, it is the most systematic argument against the ability of process thought to provide a theory of rights and justice. Second, Clark, in both his published article and his dissertation, is specifically concerned with showing that process thought violates the "common sense view of ourselves" as having "personal inviolability, equity, and rights" (Clark 1981, 133). Although my analysis is indebted to Clark's analysis in his dissertation, I have tried to limit direct quotations to published materials by Clark and Stackhouse. I am grateful to Max Stackhouse for first recommending that I take into account Clark's arguments.

2. See S.I. Benn "Justice presupposes people pressing claims and justifying them by rules or standards" (1967, 298). In his dissertation Clark provides a detailed analysis and comparison of the theories of Leo Strauss and John Rawls which supports Benn's observation (1984, chaps. II and III).

3. In his criticisms of process thought, Stackhouse is not interested in defining the nature of the determinate ideal underlying justice, but mentions as alternative definitions: "God, a universal moral law, eternal forms of the True, Good and Beautiful" (1981, 109). In his dissertation, Clark points out that historically the determinate ideal has ranged from natural law's normative view of human nature to Rawls' just procedure. What all these ideals share is being "context invariant" and giving incontrovertible limits to "right order" (cf. Clark 1984, chap. IV). Stackhouse's argument, like Clark's, is that process thought can provide *no* ideal at all, much less argue for one view of a transcendent structure of reality superior to the others.

4. "Creative synthesis," a term used more by Hartshorne than by Whitehead, is for purposes of this essay interchangeable with "creative advance." I introduce the term here because it is used by Stackhouse (1981) and Clark (1981) in their criticisms of process thought.

5. Of course, one unifying purpose that may be universally assigned to the self is the aim at richness of experience or aesthetic achievement, but I will examine that category below under the critique of aesthetic satisfaction.

6. I am especially indebted to Clark's analysis in his dissertation (1984, 198 ff.) for the form and substance of the criticisms discussed in this subsection and the subsection on creative synthesis below.

7. A more precise discussion of Whitehead's and Cobb's understanding of change and creative advance would require a detailed explanation of the differences between process as the description of the creative synthesis or concrescence of an actual occasion, and the description of change as the transition between actual occasions. Process as creative synthesis refers to what occurs within the momentary concrescence of an actual occasion. To the extent that any concrescence achieves some novel synthesis, however trivial, it is a creative synthesis of experience. Change refers to the differences among occasions of experience, and can be creative (creative advance, or what Cobb calls creative transformation), decadent, or, to a limited degree, repetitious. Although the coming into to being of any occasion of experience involves an element of creative synthesis, it does not follow that the relationship among occasions is one of creative advance. One may attempt to justify identifying creative synthesis with change because creative synthesis makes change possible in the same way that momentary actual occasions make time possible. However, by making no distinction between change in general and creative advance as one sort of change, one would obfuscate the positive nature of creative advance.

8. It is also interesting to note that in analyzing the relationship between faith and justice, Schubert Ogden takes a similar position to Niebuhr's by arguing that love, as the first requirement of faith, logically necessitates justice. Ogden points out that faith as trust in and loyalty to God requires that one love as God loves, namely,

> so as to take account of all the interests affected by our action in order to realize these interests as fully as circumstances allow. Recalling, then, the classical definition of justice as giving everyone his or her due, we may summarize the argument up to this point by saying that the faith which works by love in-

evitably seeks justice and finds expression in it.
(Ogden 1985, 91)

In other words, to love as God loves implies consideration of others' interests as well as one's own. Since a person's due is the realization of his or her interests, love involves considering what is just. However, love, unlike justice, is "unbounded," because "God's love itself is subject to no bounds ... there is no creature's interest that is not also God's interest and, therefore, necessarily included in our returning love for God" (Ogden 1985, 90). Moreover, if we assume that "the social and cultural structures by which human existence is always limited are neither divine appointments nor natural givens but human creations," then the justice demanded by love is necessarily political justice whose task it is to create proper structures of social and cultural order (Ogden 1985, 91 f.).

9. I have noticed that Cobb uses the term *biotic pyramid* less in more recent writings, so that it does not even appear in *The Liberation of Life* where he develops most fully his understanding of the basis for subhuman and human rights. Here the notion is replaced by the *web of life*, which is a better image for calling attention to mutual interrelatedness. It may be that Cobb uses *biotic pyramid* less because it connotes the notion that humanity is the final apex of life, implying, on the one hand, that evolution is complete, and, on the other, that human beings are the most valuable entities in the universe. Of course, Cobb does not assume evolution is complete; nor does he assume that human beings are the most valuable entities, for only God has claim to being the most valuable of all entities. However, I use the term, with these qualifications in mind, to illustrate the relationship among levels of the capacity for rich experience to the interrelatedness of the levels.

10. These sorts of questions are raised poignantly by Clark in his dissertation. He remarks, autobiographically, that the birth of his seriously handicapped daughter made him profoundly aware that her claim upon the community for education, therapy, and well-being, must be safeguarded even if her limited capacities require a significant share of the community's resources (Clark 1984, iii). This safeguard, of course, is "rooted in an understanding of justice which implies that she has personal equity and inviolable rights as a human being, and that her flourishing, whatever it is comprised of, is protected"—a safeguard which he believes is deteriorated if her rights are correlative to her capacity for richness of experience (Clark 1984, ix).

11. Cobb does not use the term *equity* per se, although it is clear that this is what he means in his discussion of proportionate rights, as for example, when he states that "justice does not require equality. It does require that we share one another's fate" (Birch & Cobb 1981, 165).

CHAPTER FIVE

FROM ECOLOGY TO POLITICAL AND ECONOMIC LIBERATION

The previous chapter argued that Cobb's ecological ethic is able to provide the basis of a theory of rights and justice which accounts for the notions of personal inviolability and equity, while insisting that human justice also entails a notion of ecological sustainability. Hence, Cobb's emerging theory of justice both incorporates and transcends traditional and modern aspects of Western theories of justice. However, recent schools of theology which have been profoundly influenced by Marxist analysis—including political and liberation theologies—have called into question any theory of justice which does not give central consideration to the problem of political and economic oppression. Indeed, Cobb recognizes that for a number of liberation theologians most traditional Christian theories of justice have been easily used by ruling interests to protect the rights and freedoms of an elite few rather than bringing freedom and liberation to the oppressed (cf. 1985b, 131). Because Cobb takes the criticism of political and liberation theologians seriously, it is important to examine how he attempts to deal with the issue of political and economic liberation.

Process thinkers, in general, and Cobb, in particular, have argued for some time that Whiteheadian cosmology provides a strong theoretical justification for advocating liberation (cf. Brown 1981; Ogden 1979). Indeed, as I pointed out at the end of chapter three, Cobb argues that his central normative category of creative transformation embodies Freire's notion of conscientization. Moreover,

the centrality of personal inviolability in Cobb's view of justice indicates a theoretical commitment to the principle of free exercise of
individual rights. Nonetheless, it may be argued that Cobb's theoretical admiration for liberation is tainted both by his appreciation for
the esoteric cosmological theory of Whitehead, which is extremely
difficult to comprehend much less capable of leading to praxis, and by
his practical interest in the ecological crisis, which betrays a first-
world, middle-class, white male perspective that appears to give priority to an issue, which, if attended to with the energy that Cobb advocates, trivializes the radical importance of human liberation of all
sorts. The first section of this chapter briefly outlines Cobb's cosmological understanding of freedom and liberation, and then examines
and evaluates Cobb's reasons for believing that Whiteheadian cosmology, with all of its complexities, is not opposed to committed
praxis of liberation. The second section examines whether Cobb's
ecological commitment conflicts with the commitment to human
liberation. The final section offers some overall observations about
the theological and ethical significance of Christ as creative transformation for interreligious dialogue.

LIBERATION AND PRAXIS IN COBB'S THEOLOGY

COSMOLOGICAL BASIS OF FREEDOM AND LIBERATION

From what has been said in previous chapters, it is clear that
Cobb understands freedom to be present in varying degrees in all actual occasions. The freedom of actual occasions in part makes possible the capacity for transcendence, which is an essential feature of
the ecological model. However, Cobb does not see freedom as equivalent to being unconditioned by other events. Rather, freedom occurs
within the limitations imposed by the given world, so that there are
limits to transcendence. Put differently, "we are partially created by
our environment and partially self-created" (Cobb & Griffin 1976,
25). For Cobb, this means that there is always "some space" left for
freedom—although that "space" can be dramatically limited by the
causal past (1981b, 23).

Moreover, as I pointed out previously, even though
Whitehead and Cobb hold that freedom or spontaneity belongs to the
essence of actual occasions, that freedom is made possible by God's
provision of an initial ideal aim. Indeed, the presence of freedom is

enhanced to the degree that the initial ideal aim offers greater novel possibilities. In human experience, "the greater the effective presence of the Logos [Christ], the greater the human freedom in the determination of what will in fact be attained" (1975, 172). Because freedom is made possible and is enhanced by the effectiveness of Christ in one's becoming, Cobb refers to Christ or creative transformation as "the principle of liberation" (1975, 58). Conversely, freedom is limited to the extent that one is not open to creative transformation, because one is not open to the range of novel possibilities which make freedom possible.

There are numerous reasons why one may not be open to creative transformation. In general, one may not be open by reason of one's preference to repeat previous experiences of value, or one may not be open by reason of oppressive physical, social, political, and economic factors (see Cobb 1981b, 23). Because we ought to serve creative transformation, we have a fundamental responsibility to promote the sort of liberation that enhances openness to creative transformation in ourselves and others, which includes removing or limiting those things which inhibit the possibilities for self-transcendence, whether this be political oppression or self-centered consumerism. Hence, Cobb affirms that "freedom is not freedom *from* one another but freedom *for* one another" (Birch & Cobb 1981, 188).

This responsibility has important implications in the political and economic spheres. It calls for developing political and economic structures that allow all to participate as fully as possible in shaping their own destiny (see Birch & Cobb 1981, 187).

> That means that government should both encourage agency and itself be a function of such agency. This is not achieved by asking people to make decisions about matters remote from their competence and interest. It is advanced by encouraging decisions close to competence and interest and expanding the range of that competence and interest. It is unlikely to be developed when people are treated as the objects of the decisions of an elite even if these decisions are intended benevolently. (1981b, 23)

Such a view clearly places Cobb in opposition to political and economic policies and structures which support patriarchal and neo-colonial attitudes and practices, that is, all practices which inhibit growth and exercise of self-determination.

The responsibility to enhance participation entails a preference for persuasion over violence: "the merit of a social system is the extent to which it moves people by persuasion rather than by coercion" (1981b, 24). Coercion, for Cobb, is not limited to physical violence; it includes any means that discourages free and critical response, such as deceptive advertisements and propaganda. Moreover, Cobb notes that "the most important means of coercion is the economic," and credits Marxist analysis for uncovering many aspects of coercion which had formerly been hidden (1981b, 24). However, contrary to orthodox Marxism, Cobb's preference for persuasion leads him to caution against "too ready an acceptance of violence as an instrument of social change" (1981b, 27). Nevertheless, he acknowledges that coercive structures may be so oppressive and implacable that violence is justified if less violent development is unlikely, and if there is "the real possibility of a greatly superior social order being achieved through violence" (1981b, 28).

In short, Cobb's process understanding of freedom leads him to affirm many themes similar to those found in liberation theology. Freedom is not a privilege, but a metaphysical and moral necessity. We are called to work toward liberation in all areas of our lives, but particularly in the political and economic spheres where coercion often denies participation. Marxist thought has been particularly valuable in unmasking institutionalized forms of violence which have prevented participation in economic life. And, even though Cobb does not advocate violent revolution as the norm for achieving liberation, he acknowledges that it may at times be justified.

FROM COSMOLOGY TO PRAXIS

As persuasive and attractive as Cobb's account of freedom is, its validity is ultimately dependent upon a cosmology of actual occasions, eternal objects, prehensions, creative syntheses, primordial and consequent natures of deity, and so forth. Even some first-world thinkers question the necessity and value of taking on what amounts to a radically new world view, while many of those theologians concerned with the education and preparation of pastors wonder whether process theology is preachable to the average layperson. More so, liberation and political theologians question the relevance of such theorizing when the demands of praxis are so compelling. Jürgen Moltmann states the problem forcefully:

> I am not so much interested in Whitehead in regard to his process-thought and his "becoming God" with a primordial and consequent nature, though I like his phrase about God as "the great companion—the fellow-sufferer who understands." My co-suffering reason would wish to know what is going on in his divinity in relationship to those abandoned, starved, bereft of their own name and their honor, and what practical consequences follow for the philosopher and theologian. Electromagnetic fields do not interest me relative to a *religious Weltanschauung* congenial to my scientific reason, but relative to the electrification of the shacks of sharecroppers in North Carolina and the slums of Nairobi. (Moltmann 1972, 58)

To put an even finer point on the question, if the issues of justice, liberation, and sustainability can be engaged adequately within more accessible conceptualities, if process thought is not preachable, and if its theorizing diverts attention from concrete commitment to liberation of the oppressed, would it not be better theoretically, pastorally, and ethically, to abandon process thought to those with the luxury to master its intricacies and conserve our energies for more pressing problems? In short, do the cosmological subtleties of process theology prevent it from being a practical theology, particularly in the sense called for by liberation theologians? It may be that this question cannot be answered to the full satisfaction of those who have asked it. Nonetheless, I believe that one can find in Cobb's thought good reasons for arguing that process thought can be a practical theology in the conventional and radical senses of that word.

The question of whether there are more accessible conceptualities than Cobb's process thought which address issues of justice, liberation, and sustainability, in some senses can only be settled by the test of time. However, throughout this essay, I have noted Cobb's criticisms of traditional conceptualities that bear upon this question. Indeed, Cobb's earliest work is a response to the failure of

Wieman's radical empiricism and Barthian style neo-orthodoxy to relate adequately the experience of faith to intellectual belief. From the beginning, Cobb has recognized the ethical implications of this failure: Wieman's empirical understanding of God tends to weaken and potentially to undermine meaningful loyalty to the source of human good; Barth's radical separation of faith from belief tends to undermine rational consideration of the implications of faith for life (cf. Cobb 1962, chaps. 1 & 2). Hence, these two conceptualities do not appear capable of sustaining an adequate practical theology.

It may be argued that Reinhold Niebuhr's work, on the one hand, and political and liberation theologies, on the other, do offer more accessible conceptualities which adequately address issues of justice, liberation, and sustainability. Cobb's general criticism of Niebuhr's theology and German political theology, is that their conceptualities are fundamentally anthropocentric, and consequently, incapable of adequately dealing with the issue of sustainability (cf. 1981b, 12 f.; 1982b, 111 ff.). Even if one accepts the questionable position that ecological sustainability is either of secondary importance to justice and liberation or can be addressed solely in terms of what serves human well-being, the conceptualities of both schools of thought tend to understand justice and liberation in terms of first-world standards of economic development measured by per capita gross national product, industrialization, and urbanization—all of which have negative implications for third world justice and liberation (cf. 1981b, 13; 1982b, 120 ff.; Birch & Cobb 1981, 236 ff.). In particular, Cobb points out that the presupposed world views of both Niebuhr and the German political theologians assume a dichotomy between history and nature which tends to associate human social change with history, and history with "economic progress, urban development, and industrialization" (1981b, 13; 1982b, 120). To illustrate his point, Cobb points out that history is generally written by urban people about urban events; whereas, rural life is viewed as remote and backwards, and a subject of anthropologists, not historians. Indeed, *political* theology tends to be a theology of the *polis* or city, not of the subsistence farmer (1982b, 120).

The tendency to identify human liberation with per capita gross national product, industrialization, and urbanization ignores the non-economic factors essential to true liberation such as infant mortality, life expectancy, and literacy, which are better measured by the

Physical Quality of Life Index proposed by the U.S. Overseas Development Council (Birch & Cobb 1981, 237). Cobb notes, for example, that Iran, which was industrialized under the Shah, had a per capita income of $1250, while at the same time rural Sri Lanka had a per capita income of only $130. Nevertheless, on the 100 point scale of the Physical Quality of Life Index (100 being the highest score), Sri Lanka ranked 83, compared to Iran's mere 38 (Birch & Cobb 1981, 236 f.). Too often, policies which emphasize industrialization and urbanization disrupt social and family life, denigrate rural people as backward, and reduce the economic status of women who, before industrialization, usually are responsible for most of the day to day food production (1982b, 120). Indeed, the transition to a money economy has "often encouraged the shift from raising food for local consumption to growing cash crops for export," so that land owner- ship shifts to the hands of the few, and malnutrition becomes a problem (1982b, 120 f.). In short, Cobb's point in these criticisms is not that Niebuhrian and political theologies tend to cause injustice and oppression; but rather, they do not offer conceptualities which counter these tendencies (1981b, 13).

Cobb is more amenable to feminist, Black, and third world liberation theologies. In part, this seems to be a result of Cobb's recognition that his social location makes it difficult to be critical of theologies emerging from feminist, Black, and third-world per- spectives. In part, the growing interaction among these various lib- eration theologies is responsible for an emerging "paradigm" or world view that has much in common with Cobb's ecological model (1983b, 5). In particular, feminist theologians, such as Rosemary Radford Ruether, have made important strides in recognizing the in- terrelationships among the oppression of women, Blacks, third-world peoples, and the sub-human world (see Ruether, 1975). Moreover, some of the early work of feminists such as Mary Daly (1973) indi- cates that feminism has some congeniality with Whiteheadian conceptuality.

Nonetheless, Cobb does believe that there are some theoretical weaknesses in liberation theology that might be corrected by critical appropriation of process thought. For example, Cobb does find it important, in the spirit of dialogue, to question the widely prevalent tendencies among many liberation theologians to appropriate uncrit- ically Marxism as the only alternative to capitalism (1985b, 131), and

to view hermeneutics as "the foundational or even encompassing theological task" (1983b, 5 f.). In particular, Cobb finds it questionable
that only one "economic-political system can be the one and final
goal for the human race," or that all human history can be reduced to
economic causes, for, in neither case is there a recognition of
pluralism in achievements of civilization and in the roots of injustice
(1981b, 17). Moreover, to focus too much on interpretation of biblical texts that speak to one's particular context, as Latin American
theologians do, without global awareness of "the life and death issues
of our time," can leave unquestioned such issues as sexism and anti-
Judaism that are found in many of the biblical texts (1983b, 6).

The question of whether Cobb's process thought is
"preachable," and thus relevant to those in the Christian church who
most need to be empowered to lead lives of liberating praxis, is also a
question that only time can answer fully. However, Cobb is keenly
aware that the efficacy of even a "politicized" process theology depends upon its ability to "claim the center" of the self-understanding
of the church. Indeed, Cobb notes that in the United States, not only
process theologians, but all "theological faculties, have, on the
whole, moved from the center to the periphery of the thought-life of
the church" (1986a, 3). Cobb believes that this move to the periphery of the church's thinking about itself and its mission is a result
of theologians' growing self-understanding that theology and ethics
are discrete academic disciplines, serving the interests of an academic
community, rather than life and faith (1986a, 5). Cobb commends
liberation theologians as the best examples of moving towards the
center because they "direct attention to the real world rather than to the
advancement of a discipline" (1986a, 6). Cobb's own shift in theological method toward "global Christian thinking" represents his own
effort to move toward claiming the center.

Nonetheless, one might wonder how even global Christian
thinking can claim the center if it is indebted to a cosmological theory
that many find extremely complex, if not arcane. To a certain degree,
this difficulty has faced most major theological movements, even
those which, at one time or another, have claimed the center: accessibility to neo-orthodoxy requires some comprehension of the vocabulary of existentialism; accessibility to Latin American liberation
theology requires some comprehension of the vocabulary of Marxist
theory. So too, accessibility to process theology will require some

understanding of basic Whiteheadian concepts. In this regard, Cobb and other process thinkers are making concrete efforts to make process conceptuality more accessible, for example, by the founding of *Faith and Process*, a center specifically designed to relate process theology in a non-academic way to the life of the church. More importantly, Cobb's recognition of the importance of images in theological discourse, particularly the image of Christ as creative transformation and the ecological model, points toward a vocabulary that is more "preachable," while conveying the implications of a theology informed by Whiteheadian cosmology. There is certainly more that needs to be done in this area before Cobb's process theology can hope to affect more fully the life of the church. However, the fact that Cobb is already moving in this direction indicates that the obstacle of Whitehead's complex conceptuality is not necessarily insurmountable.[1]

Moreover, if Cobb is correct that the crucial issues of our time require a fundamental shift in character to a new form of Christian existence, then there does need to be a corresponding shift in world view which will require a new conceptuality. This, I believe, is a radical and long term proposal implicit in Cobb's theology. Such a shift may not enable process theology to be assimilated immediately into the life of the church. But no paradigm shift ever has been accomplished quickly.

The question whether the theoretical nature of Cobb's thought diverts attention away from the more immediate needs of liberating praxis is part of the larger debate over the proper relationship between theory and praxis. Cobb has great sympathy with the claim of liberation theologians that theory ought to serve praxis, and he confesses that process thought has too often neglected the demands of praxis for the sake of developing theory (see 1982b, vii; 1985b, 126). Moreover, to the extent that liberation theologies are converging upon a conceptuality that is at least partly worked out by Cobb's process theology, there seems to be good reason for believing that process thought is capable of being a theology of praxis.

Cobb's own reflection on the debate over the relationship between praxis and theory attempts to overcome the dualistic, either/or character of the debate while recognizing the criticisms of praxis-oriented theologies. Cobb acknowledges that all thinking is socially conditioned, that is, thinking "emerges in an experience that is the product of myriads of causes, and it is inevitably affected by those causes" (1983b, 1). Hence, Cobb recognizes that there is no theory completely free of ideological influences. However, Cobb also affirms that genuine thinking "has some element of creativity, autonomy, or transcending. That which is simply the outcome of antecedent conditions is not thinking" (1983b, 1). Hence, Cobb rejects both the contention that theory is completely free of ideological conditionedness and the contention that theory is completely determined by ideology.

The question, then, for Cobb's process theology is whether it attempts to serve liberating praxis, or whether it serves, albeit unconsciously, an ideology of oppression. If Cobb is correct, as I believe he is, that "reflection on how one's thinking is determined can expand the range of freedom by breaking, in principle, the power of the conditions which, when unrecognized, hold unquestioned sway" (1983b, 1), then Cobb's theoretical reflection demonstrates growing conscientization, and hence commitment to liberating praxis. However, Cobb admits that as a first-world, white, male theologian, he thinks and speaks from the social location of the dominant society "which share[s] in sustaining and strengthening the structures of oppression and destruction which govern our world" (1982b, 15). Hence, Cobb recognizes that he cannot become a liberation theologian who, by definition, speaks from the social location of oppression. Nonetheless, like the political theologians of Europe, Cobb is willing to enter into self-critical dialogue with liberation theologians, and thereby to transform process theology into a political theology (1982b, 15; 1985b, 124 ff.).

The next section examines how faithful Cobb is to this process of conscientization, but it is worth noting briefly how Cobb's theory can accommodate the interests of liberating praxis. One might think that Cobb's theoretical commitment to the notion of organic interrelatedness would lead him to welcome and encourage the present state of global interdependence, particularly economic and technological interdependence, as a means toward international understanding and cooperation. However, as the previous chapter indicated, Cobb recognizes that there are both good and bad forms of interrelatedness. In applying the ecological model to the issue of the present state of global interdependence, interrelatedness is promoted insofar as it contributes to the attainment of intrinsic value and enhances opportunities for transcendence. Cobb points out that present forms of global interdependence function as a means to further domination, that is, as.a means of inhibiting the rights and freedoms which make possible achievements of intrinsic value and transcendence. For example, struggling nations who attempt to develop economically by participating in international trade, in their effort to be competitive must often limit freedoms and rights, such as unionization, which might raise the cost of domestic production and thus harm their competitiveness in the international market (1983a, 14). Moreover, present forms of global interdependence are even harmful to possibilities for increased interrelatedness. For example, the interdependence of the United States and the Middle East, created by the United States' need for oil and the Middle East's need for economic and technological development, has not led, on the part of United States citizens "to enlightened and compassionate concern for the people of the Middle East" despite the educational and cultural exchanges that have accompanied growing interdependence (1983a, 13). Rather, there are growing efforts to "defend" United States' interests in the Middle East, even to the point of increased military presence in the region.

In both examples, Cobb's theoretical standpoint enables him to recognize that global interdependence has furthered domination of the powerful over the weak rather than a cooperation that empowers all. Hence, for our time, Cobb urges that efforts should be turned away from increasing interdependence, and toward removing domination by advocating self-sufficiency, especially among struggling nations. In short, Cobb's ecological model, with its emphasis upon the possibilities of transcendence and intrinsic value of individuals as well as interrelatedness, already moves in the direction called for by liberation. However, for Cobb, liberating praxis must include not only efforts to transform activities and structures which obstruct human liberation, but also those activities and structures which deny the liberation of life everywhere, including the subhuman world. This divergence from liberation and political theologies leads to the next section.

ECOLOGICAL LIBERATION VERSUS POLITICAL AND ECONOMIC LIBERATION

Cobb certainly believes that there is no inherent conflict between an ecological theology and a political or liberation theology. In *The Liberation of Life*, Cobb states that he and Birch chose the term *liberation* to touch upon what is common to all liberation movements—sexual, racial, political, economic, and ecological—namely, the call to overcome all oppressive structures and ideologies (Birch & Cobb 1981, 1). At the "deepest roots" of all forms of oppression Cobb discerns unquestioned images and paradigms that unconsciously support a basic disposition to view "the other"—whether it be the non-human or anyone who is not part of one's group—as an object (Birch & Cobb 1981, 1 f.). To trust and serve Life, in the sense elaborated in chapter three, means to view all creatures for what they are in themselves and for God, which leads not only to ecological sustainability, but also political liberation (cf. 1985b, 138; Birch & Cobb 1981, 187). Hence, Cobb believes that process theology can move "toward a role complementary of that of liberation theology" (1985b, 124), and, indeed, "process theology ought to become a political theology," particularly in the sense of Dorothee Sölle's affirmation that a political theology calls for nothing less than commitment to "the indivisible salvation of the whole world" (1982b, 15).

In *Process Theology as Political Theology*, Cobb notes that some political theologians, such as Moltmann, are moving toward the view that the subhuman is not a mere means to human historical achievement, but has "its own rights and equilibria" (1982b, 111, quoting Moltmann 1974, 334). However, Cobb acknowledges that some political theologians, such as Johann Baptist Metz, might object that enlarging the horizon of political theology to include ecological ethics would prevent it from speaking adequately to the issue of human liberation (1982b, 112). The question then is, does the ecological commitment of Cobb's process theology compete with the commitment to political and economic liberation of political theology, and a fortiori of liberation theologies?

This question continues the discussion begun in the previous chapter where it was asked whether justice and sustainability are competitive goals. There it was briefly noted that a vision of a just world implied a vision of a sustainable world. However, the question of compatibility between the goal of political and economic liberation, on the one hand, and ecological sustainability, on the other, carries the discussion a step further because improvements in the distribution of resources and the safeguarding of the environment can be achieved as much through oppressive measures as through measures which promote human liberation. For example, the policies of Maoist China, such as the cultural revolution and the strict limitation on the number of offspring per couple, have contributed to both justice and sustainability by creating greater educational and economic equality as well as by curbing China's population explosion. However, the cost of such achievements—achievements which Cobb recognizes as laudable—has been totalitarianism (cf. Birch & Cobb 1981, 314). Hence, the question of liberation challenges process theology to broaden its scope further.

This question can only be answered fully at the level of praxis. Hence, Cobb analyzes concrete situations to show that the practical goals of ecological sustainability do not take away from the practical goals of liberation, but rather the two goals converge. Cobb observes that "there is no conflict between an emphasis on the liberation of the poor and on the preservation and restoration of the land from which they and their descendants must live" (1985b, 137). The convergence of the goals of human political and economic liberation, on the one hand, and the goals of the liberation of the subhuman world, on the other, can be seen most persuasively in Cobb's analysis of the political and economic liberation of women.

Drawing upon the insights of the feminist theologian, Rosemary Radford Ruether, Cobb observes that in Western culture women "have been traditionally identified with nature, and nature in turn has been seen as an object of domination by men" (Birch & Cobb 1981, 310). This observation appears to be borne out in the history of colonial and neo-colonial economic development, which has not only been destructive of environmental sustainability, but has also exacerbated sexual oppression. By imposing private ownership of property, which of course was limited to men, and introducing plantations for the growing of cash crops, which generally employed only men, colonialism disrupted tribal farm economies, in which women were primary food-producers and land was communally owned (Birch & Cobb 1981, 311). The disruption of tribal bonds to the land

and the introduction of cash crops has also been accompanied by deforestation and erosion of topsoil. Hence, as women have become increasingly marginalized socially and economically, even though they continue to be the primary food producers, the land, forests, and the animals living there, have been rapidly endangered. Nor have modern policies of economic development improved the lot of women or ecological sustainability. The same policies of economic development which promote urbanization and industrialization to the detriment of the environment also assume that men should have economic and political leadership, so that educational and employment opportunities—and hence, economic and political power—are made more accessible to men than women (Birch & Cobb 1981, 310 f.).

Moreover, as women lose political and economic power, the role of women becomes narrowed to that of child bearing and rearing, so that women increasingly lose rights over their own bodies, particularly the right to decide how many children they want to bear. As Cobb points out, "the great injustice which is perpetuated in this denial to women of their rights over their own bodies is also a major source of unsustainable population growth on a global scale" (Birch & Cobb 1981, 314). Thus, oppression of women adds directly to the oppression of the environment. Conversely, the political and economic liberation of women can do much to liberate the environment. As women become full participants in the economic and political arenas through educational and employment opportunities, they will have greater personal freedom, and "study after study has shown that when women have real freedom to choose they opt for fewer children," which thus alleviates pressure upon sustainability (1982b, 131).

Of course, even with increased educational and employment opportunities and greater rights over their own bodies, women are often still subjected to oppression. Indeed, in the United States, where there have been great strides in these areas, there remains a great deal of injustice to women. For example, "the pace at which the earning gap between women and men is being narrowed in the United States is so slow that at this rate of change, women's salaries will converge with men's in about 2500 years" (Birch & Cobb 1981, 315)! Moreover, much of the continued oppression of women in the first world can be linked to many men's view of women as consumer objects to be competed for and possessed. This consumer attitude toward women also contributes to the sort of wasteful consumption which threatens ecological sustainability:

> With reduced roles as parent and homemaker, and denied equal opportunity in the earning of money and the satisfaction of professional life, [women] are encouraged to devote themselves to beautification of self and homes according to carefully manipulated norms. Men are similarly led to identify their masculinity with the driving of heavy, inefficient cars and to attract women through large expenditures on unnecessary objects. (Birch & Cobb 1981, 316)

Hence, the factors which reduce women to the status of commodities also lead to a depletion of personal, economic, and physical resources. Cobb suggests that insofar as "women and men relate to one another more fully as persons, one major prop of the wasteful consumer society in which we now live will be removed" (Birch & Cobb 1981, 316).

In addition, Cobb argues that the liberation of women is required to ensure a sustainable world, not only because the liberation of women will lead to slower population growth and a lessening of consumerism, but also because "women can help develop the new attitudes toward the non-human world" (Birch & Cobb 1981, 317 f.). The cultural and economic realities which have supported both the domination of women by men and the domination of the subhuman world by humanity, have contributed to women being, on the whole, "more aware of the interconnectedness of human life with the rest of nature," and, hence, women have the sorts of sensitivities that "are those needed by society if it is to reverse the directions of destructive 'development' and to attain justice and sustainability" (Birch & Cobb 1981, 317). Therefore, women are peculiarly qualified to provide leadership in making the sorts of changes which will ensure sustainability.

It should be clear that Cobb's analysis not only points to a convergence of the goals of ecological liberation with women's liberation, but also with third world liberation. The sorts of political and economic policies and structures which destroy the environment and deny freedom to women are characterized by urbanization and industrialization, which we have seen, has led to the concentration of land ownership in the hands of a few and diminished the ability of third world countries to feed themselves. However, Cobb realizes that the convergence of ecological theology and liberation theology is not always a perfect coincidence of interests. For example,

> Land-hungry peasants in Africa want to cultivate areas that are reserved for wild animals which they are for-bidden to hunt. Indeed, in the short run there can be little doubt that the poor could profit from the slaughter of the remaining elephants by selling the ivory and farming the land. (1985b, 138)

But Cobb argues that when people realize that short term gains will impoverish their children, they will seek other solutions to their plight. Cobb trusts that there will be "far fewer instances in which there is marked opposition between the interests of the poor and of the whole biosphere" when we transcend a "trade-off" mentality which assumes, a priori, that human liberation is inevitably at odds with the liberation of the non-human environment (see 1985b, 139). For Cobb, trust in Christ as creative transformation entails that we must begin with the assumption that justice, liberation, and sustainability serve one another.

It is important to add that Cobb's vision of a just, liberated, sustainable world does not entail a repudiation of all urban and indus-trial achievements and a return to primitive or rural life. Although Cobb is harshly critical of the urban-industrial ideal as a model for development, he recognizes that large portions of the world are so dependent upon urban-industrial civilization, that to attempt to return to a simpler life would lead to wide-spread suffering (see Birch & Cobb 1981, 171). The vision of a just, liberated, and sustainable world takes a variety of forms, relevant to given conditions. Hence, where human life is already vitally dependent upon urbanization and industrialization, Cobb advocates the transformation of city and in-dustry, such as that proposed by Paolo Soleri, so as to provide urban-industrial centers which have minimal impact upon the environment (see chap. three). At the same time, Cobb points out that those of us living in the urbanized first-world have ignored the fact that large por-tions of the world's human population live in rural, peasant cultures. Cobb calls us to recognize and respect the value of these cultures, as

well as to work toward their advancement in ways that do not assume
that either their interests or the interests of the subhuman world must
be sacrificed for the sake of the other.

Lest Cobb's call be misunderstood, Cobb is in no way suggesting that justice, liberation, and sustainability are to be attained by
maintaining the advantages of urban-industrial civilization at the expense of rural civilization—such is the present state of affairs, even
where efforts are made to urbanize and industrialize rural civilizations.
Rather, a transformed urban-industrial civilization will mean a cur-
tailment on consumption and production of wealth; whereas a transformed rural civilization will allow for sustainable growth to provide
more than mere food and shelter, but also improved transportation,
greater economic opportunities for women, improved health and medical care, and increased literacy and education (see Birch & Cobb 1981,
237, chap. 10).

CONCLUDING REFLECTIONS

Throughout this essay, I have indicated areas of John Cobb's
thought which I believe offer a solid basis for theological ethics, as
well as areas which I believe need further refinement and elaboration.
On the whole, I believe that Cobb's process theology provides a rich
resource for Christian social ethics. Undoubtedly, one of Cobb's
most important contributions to Christian social ethics is a conceptuality that both challenges and allows Christians to recognize the
value of the non-human world to itself and to God, and hence
Christians' responsibility to safeguard and promote it. Of all the
major Christian theologians on the American scene today, Cobb
stands alone in his prophetic call that faithfulness to Christ entails an
ecological responsibility which is not separable from dedication to
human justice and liberation. Indeed, like another John of ages past,
John Cobb is a voice crying in the wilderness that Christ is indeed
present there.

I have argued that at the heart of Cobb's mature theological
ethics is his view of Christ as creative transformation, and hence I
have characterized Cobb's ethics as christocentric. However, it is
important to reiterate that Christ as creative transformation is not a
monolithic or exclusivistic ideal, theologically or ethically. For if it
is acknowledged that Christ is the universally creative, transforming

activity of God, then conformity to Christ makes it possible to be transformed by other competing ideals. Indeed, as pointed out in chapter three, Cobb's own openness to Latin American and feminist liberation ideals of Christ has led him to creatively transform the meaning of his own ideal of Christ.

More significantly, the call for openness to creative transformation by other ideals extends beyond the confines of other christologies and makes possible openness to transformation by other religious Ways. This possibility was alluded to briefly in chapter three, where it was noted that Cobb's dialogue with Buddhism contributed to his post-1969 revision of the meaning of love as both *agape* and compassion. However, I believe that, for Cobb, openness to transforming dialogue with other religious Ways is not merely made possible by a christology of Christ as creative transformation; rather openness to other Ways is theologically and morally required by his christology. That is, loyalty to and trust in Christ as creative transformation calls for "submitting all that one believes to radical questioning and opening oneself critically to alien ideas" (1982a, 46). To that end, Cobb argues that there needs to be more attention to interreligious dialogue.

Although it is beyond the scope of an essay in theological ethics to elaborate how Cobb envisions transforming dialogues with other Ways (see Cobb 1982a for his discussion of the subject), I do want at least to indicate briefly that far from detracting from Cobb's Christian social ethics, the call to interreligious dialogue can contribute significantly to it. It might be argued that interreligious dialogue is a first-world luxury, and hence, diverts attention away from liberation of the two-thirds world. However, most persons of the two-thirds world are not Christian and find little even in a Christian liberation theology that is relevant to their own situation. Interreligious dialogue among Christian liberation theologians and their oppressed sisters and brothers who are Muslim, Buddhist, Confucian, and so forth, can open all parties to deeper insights into the nature and extent of oppression and, conversely, liberation. Cobb notes, for example that Minjung theology in Korea is finding in the "study of Shamanism, Confucianism, and Buddhism, . . . ways in which Christian faith can be appropriately expressed" in relation to the *minjung* or common people (1985b, 134). Moreover, I suggest that interreligious dialogue may also contribute to a more adequate re-

sponse to the ecological crisis both by promoting intercultural understanding that can lead to international cooperation, and by mutually
broadening each tradition's understanding of humanity's relationship
to the subhuman world.

In closing, it is worth noting how Cobb's christocentrism
expresses a fundamental confidence in the possibility that op-
positions—whether of religious ways or of competing ethical principles—can become contrasting elements in a novel synthesis that
preserves the integrity of those elements. Put differently, for Cobb,
faith in Christ entails confidence that conflicting aims and goals can
often become mutually supportive. This confidence may be the most
controversial aspect of Cobb's theory of rights, justice, and liberation.
Some may find Cobb's belief that the demands of human justice,
human liberation, and planetary sustainability, can be mutually supportive is ultimately naive because humanity will destroy itself and
the planet before it can make much headway in resolving these issues
in any holistic way. Yet it should be clear from what has been said
above, that Cobb harbors no naive hopes that humanity will avoid
global destruction. The openness of the future and the freedom of
human beings are such that God's providential care cannot prevent
humanity's self-destruction if it chooses to stay its present course.
However, God's providence is not without efficacy, and naive hope is
not the same as a realistic hope that our present situation can be creatively transformed. I think that many of Cobb's examples of how
conflicting goals can become mutually supportive provide grounds for
believing that creative transformation is a reality. And the reality of
God's creative transformative activity—the reality of Christ—does
provide a basis for measured hope that humanity can avoid planetary
disaster. However, whether this reality has the final say, even if
humanity destroys the world entrusted to it, does indeed seem to be, in
the last analysis, a matter of faith. This sort of faith Whitehead calls
"Peace," the "Harmony of Harmonies," the "trust in the self-justi-
fication of Beauty," which only "comes as a gift" (Whitehead 1933,
285). This faith underlies Cobb's entire theological ethics.

NOTES

1. It is interesting to note that Cobb has also written in areas that one might call "preachable." He has contributed a volume on *Theology and Pastoral Care* (1977b) to Howard Clinebell's series, *Creative Pastoral Care and Counseling Series*. Without becoming too technical, this book applies notions such as the Christian structure of existence to counseling, and even offers a chapter on developing a vocabulary that translates biblical conceptuality into a more theologically precise, yet accessible, language. He has also written two short works on prayer for the devotional publishers, The Upper Room. The first, *To Pray or Not to Pray* (1974), is a personal account of Cobb's own questions and experiences of prayer. The second, *Praying for Jennifer* (1985c), is a fictionalized account of some teenagers' experience with intercessory prayer. All three of these books attempt to bridge the gap between common language and Whiteheadian conceptuality in dealing with practical issues likely to emerge in middle-class American, Christian experience.

REFERENCES

Altizer, T. J. J.
1971   Dialectical vs. di-polar theology. *Process Studies* 1: 29-37.

Ayer, A. J.
1952   *Language, truth and logic.* New York: Dover Publications.

Beardslee, W. A.
1972   *A house for hope: A study in process and biblical thought.* Philadelphia: Westminster Press.

Belaief, L.
1984   *Toward a Whiteheadian ethics.* Lanham, MD: University Press of America.

Benn, S. I.
1967   Justice. In *The encyclopedia of philosophy*, edited by P. Edwards, Vol. 4, 298-302. New York: Macmillan Publishing Co.

Birch, C., & Cobb, J. B.
1981   *The liberation of life: From the cell to the community.* London: Cambridge University Press.

Brown, D.
1981   *To set at liberty.* Maryknoll, NY: Orbis Books.

Brown, D., James, R. E., & Reeves, G.
1971   *Process philosophy and Christian thought.* Indianapolis: Bobbs-Merrill Educational Publishing.

Clark, H. W.
1981   Process thought and justice. In *Process philosophy
                    and social thought,* edited by J. B. Cobb, Jr., and W.
                    W. Schroeder, 132-140. Chicago: Center for the
                    Scientific Study of Religion.
1984   Dimensions of justice and process thought. Ph.D.
                    diss., Boston College.

Cobb, J. B., Jr.
1953a   The independence of Christian faith from speculative
                    beliefs. Ph.D. diss., University of Chicago.
1953b   Theological data and method. *Journal of Religion*
                    33: 212-223.
1954   The possibility of a universal normative ethic.
                    Ethics 65: 55-61.
1959   The philosophic grounds of moral responsibility: a
                    comment on Matson and Niebuhr. *Journal of Phil-
                    osophy* 56: 619-621.
1960   *Varieties of protestantism.* Philadelphia: West-
                    minster Press.
1962   *Living options in protestant theology: A survey of
                    methods.* Philadelphia: Westminster Press.
1964   Whitehead's philosophy and a Christian doctrine of
                    man. *Journal of Bible and Religion* July: 209-220.
1965a   *A Christian natural theology: Based on the thought
                    of Alfred North Whitehead.* Philadelphia: West-
                    minster Press.
1965b   Ontology, history and Christian faith. *Religion in
                    Life* 34: 270-287.
1965c   Personal christology. Center for Process Studies.
                    Photocopy.
1966   The finality of Christ in a Whiteheadian perspective.
                    In *The finality of Christ,* edited by Dow Kirkpatrick,
                    122-154. Nashville, TN: Abingdon Press.
1967a   Experienced evil and the power of God. Paper read
                    at Colgate Rochester Divinity School.
1967b   *The structure of Christian existence.* New York:
                    Seabury Press.
1969a   Bible, revelation, and Christian doctrine. Center for
                    Process Studies. Photocopy.

1969b   *God and the world*. Philadelphia: Westminster Press.

1969c   What is alive and what is dead in empirical theology? In *The future of empirical theology*, edited by B. E. Meland, 89-101. Chicago: University of Chicago Press.

1972a   The future work of Jesus. Lecture given for the Dr. Thomas White Currie Lectures at Austin Presbyterian Theological Seminary.

1972b   *Is it too late? A theology of ecology*. Beverly Hills, CA: Bruce.

1973   *Liberal Christianity at the crossroads*. Philadelphia: Westminster Press.

1974   *To pray or not to pray*. Nashville: The Upper Room.

1975   *Christ in a pluralistic age*. Philadelphia: Westminster Press.

1977a   Responses to critiques. In *John Cobb's theology in process*, edited by D. R. Griffin and T. J.J. Altizer, 150-192. Philadelphia: Westminster Press.

1977b   *Theology and pastoral care*. Philadelphia: Fortress Press.

1978   Beyond anthropocentrism in ethics and religion. In *On the fifth day,* edited by R. Morris and Michael Fox, 137-153. Washington, DC: Arcopolis Books.

1979   Christian existence in a world of limits. *Environmental Ethics* Summer: 149-158.

1980   Process theology and environmental issues. *The Journal of Religion* 60: 440-458.

1981a   A critical view of inherited theology. In *Theologians in transition*, edited by J. M. Wall, 74-81. New York: Crossroad Publishing Company.

1981b   The political implications of Whitehead's philosophy. In *Process philosophy and social thought,* edited by J. B. Cobb, Jr., and W. W. Schroeder, 11-28. Chicago: Center for the Scientific Study of Religion.

1982a   *Beyond dialogue: Toward a mutual transformation of Christianity and Buddhism.* Philadelphia: Fortress Press.

1982b   *Process theology as political theology.* Philadelphia: Westminster Press.

1983a   Envisioning a just and peaceful world. Center for Process Studies. Photocopy.

1983b   Liberation and peace: Comments by a "process" theologian. Paper read at Liberation Theology Working Group of the American Academy of Religion Annual Meeting.

1985a   Authentic existence in Christian Whiteheadian perspective. Paper read at the American Academy of Religion Annual Meeting.

1985b   Points of contact between process theology and liberation theology in matters of faith and justice. *Process Studies* 14 (no. 2): 124-141.

1985c   *Praying for Jennifer.* Nashville: The Upper Room.

1985d   Theology: From an enlightenment discipline to global Christian thinking. Published in German translation as "Theologie Von einen Aufklärungswissenschaft zu einen globalen christlichen Denken" in *Entwürfe der Theologie,* edited by J. B. Bauer, 15-40. Graz, Austria.

1986a   Claiming the center. *Criterion,* Winter: 2-8.

1986b   Ethics, religion and Christian faith. Manuscript submitted for publication (originally given in 1970 at Catholic University of America).

1986c   Process and normative ethics. Manuscript submitted for publication (originally given in 1970 at Catholic University of America).

1987   Christ beyond creative transformation. In S. T. Davis (Ed.), *Encountering Jesus: A debate on christology.* Philadelphia: Fortress Press. [Davis' book was published in 1988, just as the present work was going to press; thus, page numbers refer to photocopy of the unpublished manuscript].

Cobb, J. B., Jr., & Gier, N.
1970   Introduction. In *The theology of Altizer: Critique and response*, edited by J. B. Cobb, Jr., 13-44. Philadelphia: Westminster Press.

Cobb, J. B., Jr., & Griffin, D. R.
1976   *Process theology: An introductory exposition.* Philadelphia: Westminster Press.

Cobb, J. B., Jr., & Schroeder, W. W.
1981   *Process philosophy and social thought.* Chicago: Center for the Scientific Study of Religion.

Daly, M.
1973   *Beyond God the father: Toward a philosophy of women's liberation.* Boston: Beacon Press.
1977   The courage to leave: a response to John Cobb's theology. In *John Cobb's theology in process*, edited by D. R. Griffin and T. J. J. Altizer, 150-192. Philadelphia: Westminster Press.

Frankena, W. K.
1973   *Ethics* (2nd ed.). Englewood Cliffs, NJ: Prentice-Hall.

Gamwell, F.
1981   A discussion of John B. Cobb, Jr., "The political implications of Whitehead's Philosophy." In *Process philosophy and social thought,* edited by J. B. Cobb, Jr., and W. W. Schroeder, 11-28. Chicago: Center for the Scientific Study of Religion.

Griffin, D. R.
1976   *God, power, and evil: A process theodicy.* Philadelphia: Westminster Press.

Gustafson, J. M.
1968   *Christ and the moral life.* Chicago: University of Chicago Press.

Hartshorne, C.
1948   *The divine relativity.* New Haven, CN: Yale.
1962   *The logic of perfection.* LaSalle, IL: Open Court Publishing Company.

1965   *Anselm's discovery: a re-examination of the onto-
             logical argument for God's existence.* LaSalle, IL:
             Open Court Publishing Company.
1967   *A natural theology for our time.* LaSalle, IL: Open
             Court Publishing Company.
1970   *Creative synthesis and philosophic method.*
             London: SCM Press.

MacIntyre, A.
1981   *After virtue.* Notre Dame, IN: University of Notre
             Dame Press.

McCann, D. P.
1982   *Christian realism and liberation theology: Practical
             theologies in creative conflict.* Maryknoll, NY:
             Orbis Books.

Moltmann, J.
1972   Response to the opening presentations. In *Hope and
             the future of man*, edited by E. H. Cousins, 55-59.
             Philadelphia: Fortress Press.
1974   *The crucified God.* Translated by R. A. Wilson and
             J. Bowden. New York: Harper & Row, Publishers.

Niebuhr, R.
1943   *The nature and destiny of man, volume II.* New
             York: Charles Scribner's Sons.

Ogden, S. M.
1961   *Christ without myth.* Dallas, TX: SMU Press.
1966   *The reality of God and other essays.* San Francisco:
             Harper & Row, Publishers.
1971   A Christian natural theology? In *Process phil-
             osophy and Christian thought*, edited by D. Brown,
             R. E. James, Jr., & G. Reeves, 111-115). Indian-
             apolis: Bobbs-Merrill Educational Publishing.
             (Original essay published in 1965).
1979   *Faith and freedom: Toward a theology of liberation.*
             Nashville: Abingdon Press.
1982   *The point of christology.* San Francisco: Harper
             and Row, Publishers.
1985   The metaphysics of faith and justice. *Process
             Studies* 14 (no. 2): 87-101.

Rawls, J.
1971   *A theory of justice.* Cambridge, MA: The Belknap
                Press of Harvard University Press.

Ruether, R. R.
1975   *New woman, new earth: Sexist ideologies and hu-
                man liberation.* New York: Seabury Press.

Reynolds, C. H.
1977   Somatic ethics: Joy and adventure in the embodied
                moral life. In *John Cobb's theology in process,*
                edited by D. R. Griffin and T. J. J. Altizer, 116-132.
                Philadelphia: Westminster Press.

Stackhouse, M.L.
1981   The perils of process: A response to Sturm. In
                Process philosophy and social thought , edited by J.
                B. Cobb, Jr., and W. W. Schroeder, 103-112.
                Chicago: Center for the Scientific Study of
                Religion.

Sturm, D.
1981   Process thought and political theory: Implications
                of a principle of internal relations. In *Process
                philosophy and social thought* , edited by J. B.
                Cobb, Jr., and W. W. Schroeder, 81-102. Chicago:
                Center for the Scientific Study of Religion.

Swyhart, B.A.D.
1975   *Bioethical decision-making.* Philadelphia: Fortress
                Press.

Tracy, D.
1977   John Cobb's theological method: Interpretation and
                reflections. In *John Cobb's theology in process,*
                edited by D. R. Griffin and T. J. J. Altizer, 25-38.
                Philadelphia: Westminster Press.

Whitehead, A. N.
1925   *Science and the modern world.* New York: The
                Free Press, Macmillan Publishing Company.
1926   *Religion in the making.* New York: Meridian
                Books, New American Library.
1933   *Adventures of ideas.* New York: The Free Press,
                Macmillan Publishing Company.

1938   *Modes of thought.* New York: The Free Press, Macmillan Publishing Company.

1978   *Process and reality,* corrected edition of 1929 work, edited by D. R. Griffin and D. W. Sherburne. New York: Free Press, Macmillan Publishing Company.

Wieman, H. N.

1946   *The Source of Human Good.* Carbondale, IL: Southern Illinois University Press.

1963   Intellectual autobiography of Henry Nelson Wieman. In *The empirical theology of Henry Nelson Wieman,* edited by R. W. Bretall, 1-18. New York: MacMillan Publishing Company.

Williams, D. D.

1949   *God's grace and man's hope.* New York: Harper and Brothers.

Wolf, W. J.

1958   Christ (Jesus Christ). In *Handbook of Christian theology,* edited by M. Halverson & A. A. Cohen, 46-53. Cleveland, OH: Meridian Books.

DATE DUE

APR 1 8 '91			

HIGHSMITH   #LO-45220